The Book of Sacraments
Memorial Edition
John Mann

RONIN Publishing, Inc

Berkeley , CA

The Book of Sacraments

John Mann

Book of Sacraments:
Ritual Use of Magical Plants

Copyright: 2015 by Ronin Publishing, Inc

Pbook ISBN: 978-1-57951-210-1
Ebook ISBN: 978-1-57951-212-5

Published by
RONIN Publishing, Inc.
P.O. Box 3436
Oakland, Ca 94609
www.roninpub.com

Senior Editor	Beverly Potter
Cover design	Beverly Potter
Editor	Reid Stuart

NOTICE TO READER: This memorial reissue of the John Mann's early classic: *The First Book of Sacraments of the Church of the Tree of Life,* is for archival purposes under the First Amendment of the Constitution. Written in 1970, the Work is presented with few edits such as updated laws. The Publisher does not warrant the information and the Author is in the Spirit World. Readers should confirm information with knowledgeable professionals before consuming any homemade sacrament.

Library of Congress No 2015951784
Printed in the USA.
Distributed to the trade by Publishers Group West.

Arnie Lazarus

Adam Gottlieb is one of John A. Mann's pen names. As Gottlieb, Mann wrote *Psilocybin Production, Cooking with Cannabis, Peyote and Other Psychoactive Cacti* and many others. As Mary Jane Superweed, he wrote the wildly successful *Marijuana Consumer's and Dealer's Guide.* As John Mann, he authored the best-seller, *Secrets of Life Extension*, which was also released in German and Japanese. Mann founded the 7,000-member Church of the Tree of Life, which established many legal psychoactive substances as its sacraments. He published poetry, plays, and musicals. As Rev. Jack Dancer, he wrote about social and spiritual issues.

I lost a good friend yesterday. He was about 83. His name was John A. Mann. You might have known him by other names, The Twentieth Century Alchemist, Adam Gottlieb, Reverend Jack Dancer and Maryjane Superweed, but he was born John A. Mann. He was a writer, one of the first to write about drugs, but he also wrote a book on how to cure herpes, a book on life extension, a book about how to write parodies and numerous plays. And he was self-taught.

John was a Vet, a photographer, a stage manager for the original Hungry I, responsible for the famous North beach restaurant, Enrico's (John's idea). He was even involved with a production of the Fugs in the 60's. John taught himself composing and wrote an opera.

John Mann was an original, a real piece of work. His health was going fast in the past years. He just wanted to finish some writing. I will miss my good friend. He was always generous, funny and very human and *his name was **John A. Mann.***

— Arnie Lazarus, May 29, 2015

THE FIRST BOOK
OF SACRAMENTS
OF THE
Church of The Tree of Life

a guide for the religious use of legal mind alterants

First edition of The First Book of Sacraments

Table of Contents

Background

On November 3, 1971, founder John Mann legally incorporated The Church of the Tree of Life in the state of California. This church was created in order to declare those visionary plants and drugs that had not been scheduled to be sacraments. The church hoped to shield members who used any of their stated sacraments if the government tried to make these entheogens illegal in the future, by using a "freedom of religion" defense.

In 1972, church staff produced *The First Book of Sacraments of the Church of the Tree of Life: A Guide for the Religious Use of Legal Mind Alterants.* The original edition of this book made no mention of 5-MeO-DMT. However, a 1973 booklet *Legal Highs: A Concise Encyclopedia of Legal Herbs and Chemicals with Psychoactive Properties* included 5-MeO-DMT, noting that "the Church of the Tree of Life has declared as its religious sacraments most substances in this book."

President Clinton, on Nov. 16, 1993, signed into law the Religious Freedom Restoration Act of 1993. The Act is basically the Legislative and Executive branches of the Federal government telling the Judicial branch to pull its collective head out of its collective rear end, and give freedom of religion the protection it deserves. Unfortunately, the whole thing is, to my mind, a po- litical maneuver without any monumental effect. The restoration of the compelling government interest test does very little to protect religious users of controlled substances, because when the test was in play before, the courts almost unanimously held that government has a "compelling interest" in enforcing the state and federal anti-drug laws, and that this interest justifies whatever burden may fall on the shoulders of those people using controlled substances for religious purposes.

Books by John Mann

As Mary Jane Superweed—Stone Kingdom Syndicate

Marijuana Consumers and Dealers Guide 1968
Drug Manufacturing for Fun and Profit 1969
Complete Cannabis Cultivator 1970
Herbal Highs 1970
Super Grass Growers Guide 1970
Herbal Aphrodisiacs 1971
Home Grown Highs 1972

As Adam Gottlieb—Twentieth Century Alchemist (TCA)

Legal Highs 1973
Basic Drug Manufacture 1973
Art and Science of Cooking with Cannabis 1974
Pleasures of Cocaine 1976
Sex Drugs and Aphrodisiacs 1974

As Adam Gottlieb—Kistone, TCA & Level Press

Book of Acid 1975
Psilocybin Producer's Guide 1976
*Ancient & Modern Methods of Growing
    Extraordinary Marijuana* 1975
Peyote and Other Psychoactive Cacti 1977
Cocaine Tester's Handbook 1975

And/Or Press

Secrets of Life Extension 1982

Ronin Publishing

Cooking with Cannabis
Growing the Hallucinogens
Sex Drugs & Aphrodisacs
Growing Extraordinary Marijuana
Pleasures of Cocaine
Legal Highs
Psychedelic Underground Library
Peyote & Other Psychoactive Cacti
Psilocybin Production
Cannabis Underground Library

The Book of Sacraments

Ritual Use of Magical Plants

Church of the Tree of Life

John Mann

INTRODUCTION

The most fundamental belief of the Church of the Tree of Life is that every human being has the right to do with himself whatever he pleases as long as his actions do not interfere with the rights of any other being. We believe that a person has the right to treat his ailments with any medicine he chooses, to alter his consciousness with any psychoactive agent he wishes to use, and to engage in any mode of private behavior alone or with other consenting adults. Humanity has been denied this freedom in the past, but now aware and evolving people are recognizing that it is our moral right to govern our own private lives and that it is morally unjust for any other person or organization to attempt to interfere with this right. The right of a human being to conduct his own mental, physical and spiritual journey through life without governmental hindrance or intrusion is a profoundly religious issue. His right to make use of any gifts which God or Nature has provided is likewise a religious matter.

Church of the Tree of Life

The religious function of the Church of the Tree of Life is the celebration, acceptance and use of the gifts of God and Nature. In the United States and other places many of these gifts have been outlawed. In its struggle for human rights and freedom and Church of the Tree of Life has chosen to work within the framework of the law. Therefore we cannot claim as our sacraments any gifts from God and Nature which were made illegal prior to the organization and incorporation of our Church. Other churches which attempted to do so failed. What we can do and have done is to proclaim as our sacraments all substances in the physical universe which are not presently illegal. We have done this because these are our sacraments. If at any future date any of these sacraments are declared illegal and if our members are denied their right to use these sacraments, we will have just cause for a legal battle in the courts

Freedom without knowledge and wisdom invariably leads to chaos. If we are to maintain our freedom to enjoy these sacramental gifts of Nature we must learn to use them correctly. It is the purpose of the Books of Sacraments to impart to our members and readers some of the most basic information necessary for the successful use of our sacraments.

PREFACE

The First Book of Sacraments deals primarily with the ritual use of legal mind-altering sacraments. To demonstrate the nature and significance of ritual we have made an intensive and often detailed study of the ceremonial practices of the various ethnic groups which have had the most experience with the sacraments that we have selected for discussion in this volume.

It may be assumed that after hundreds, and sometimes thousands, of years of experience with their sacraments these cultures have acquired an appreciable body of knowledge regarding the

Primitive life was rich in experience

natural laws which govern their use. While it is true that some of their practices are rooted in superstition, pointless tradition, ancestral myths, and in some cases superimposed Christianity, many more are well-founded and reflect a profound understanding of both the sacramental materials and the human psyche.

Primitive man is often rich with experience but lacking in erudition. "Civilized Western man," conversely, is often abundant with erudition but lacking in experience. To complement the information which we have garnered from these long-experienced ethnic groups, we have conducted extensive research into the botanical, chemical and pharmacological findings of the scientific world regarding these sacraments. It is really not surprising that we have found countless instances in which scientific evidence bears witness to the fact that although he lacked our sophisticated tools and techniques, primitive man aided only by his intuition and direct experience was often very keenly aware of many of the more arcane biophysical properties of his sacraments. This realization gives us cause to wonder if many of the ceremonial practices which do not appear to have any basis in reality are representative of facts which our incomplete studies have not as yet uncovered.

USE OF SACRAMENTS

The Church of the Tree of Life does not insist that its members use any of its sacraments. Nor does it specifically recommend any of these substances. The Church, therefore, cannot be held responsible for any mishaps, which may occur from the use of misuse of these materials. We have laid down guidelines for the use of these sacraments as carefully and as thoroughly as our knowledge of them allows. We have emphasized caution at all times and especially while knowledge and experiences are being acquired. The biochemistry of one person may be different from that of another. Some are allergic to substances upon which others thrive. An individual's body needs may vary at different times. Therefore we say that one day's food may be another day's poison.

When experimenting with unfamiliar substances it is wise to use very small portions at first. If there are any undesirable effects it is not advisable to continue use of that substance, especially without medical supervision. If no effects—desirable or undesirable—occur, gradual and cautious increase of the quantity may be attempted.

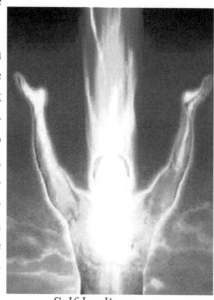

Self-healing power

The best medicine is the self-healing power of the human mind. The highest states of consciousness are those attained without the use of catalysts. Most of us have not as yet arrived at a stage of development in which we can achieve change of consciousness or healing without the aid of these substances. If the individual aspires to total freedom and independence, he may wish eventually to free himself from the need to use many of his sacraments. Therefore one should not become dependent upon these substances, but limit their use to those circumstances in which they are most meaningful.

THE VALUE OF RITUAL

Ritual is a method for organizing an experience. In the circumstances with which this book is concerned it is a tool for creating order around an inner experience. Ritual lends grace and style to actions. It helps to prevent clumsy uncertainty, wasted energy and unnecessary distractions. Because it automatically provides for all of the necessary functions within the occasion it removes the burden of concern from the conscious mind so that the individual is free to surrender himself to the experience. The use of sacraments in ritual is not inclined to degenerate into compulsive habit. Compare the ceremonial use of tobacco in the Navaho peyote rites with the nervous chain smoking of many Americans. The general

Ritual organizes experience

atmosphere and specific symbolisms of ritual help to conjure a frame of mind conducive to the experience.

The rituals described in this book are presented exactly as witnesses have reported them. We realize that most of our readers will not be able to relate strongly to many of the mythical and religious overtones, especially the heavy Roman Catholic influences among some Mexican and South American Indians. We are not trying to impose upon our members any mythical or religious beliefs. Nor are we trying to enforce any strict rules for the performance of ritual and the use of sacraments. The individual or group may follow these models precisely, use them as guidelines, or ignore them altogether. We hope that the reader, through these descriptions, will gain some insight into the essence and significance of-ritual. Then, if it is his desire, he will be able to organize his own rituals founded upon his personal beliefs and feelings.

THE USE OF MAGICAL PLANTS

When used properly mind alterants can open new channels of awareness. For the most part these altered states of awareness are temporary, but if good advantage is made of them, lasting values can be gained. This accomplishment requires some effort on the part of the individual employing these sacraments. Mind alterants cannot by themselves bring about the desired results. An analogy may be useful:

One is lost in the forest and does not know which direction will take him to the desired place. He climbs to the top of a tall tree. Here he has a commanding perspective for many miles around. In the distance he can see the desired place. If he takes his bearings and retains them as he descends once more to ground level, he may proceed in the right direction and travel a long way before he needs to check his bearings again. If he fails to establish his bearings in terms of ground-level travel, or if he loses his bearings during his descent, he may have to climb the tree once more to regain his bear-

Mind manifesting herbs can open a door to an interpersonal journey.

Mind-body harmony

ings. Some people spend years climbing the same tree or nearby ones over and over again momentarily gratifying themselves with a hazy and distant vision of the desired place, but never making any progress towards it at ground level.

Another analogous way of perceiving this situation is that if one finds a key to a door which has previously barred his progress, he does not stand there repeatedly inserting the key in the keyhole, opening and closing the door. Instead he passes through the doorway and journeys on to meet new doors and discover new keys.

To gain the greatest benefits from a journey into altered states of consciousness one should understand the nature and structure of the experience. Many mind alterants elicit a state of awareness in which the conscious intellectual processes are temporarily reduced while the more subconscious and intuitive realizations are amplified. Because the intellectual and nonintellectual spheres of awareness are so vastly different for most of us it is often difficult to comprehend what has been realized in one after returning to the other. The most natural way to overcome this problem is to take advantage of that twilight zone or middle ground between the two spheres which is usually experienced during the return journey. An example of how this middle ground is used may be observed in the peyote rites of the Navaho:

The first period of the ceremony is intended for feeling and experiencing. After the hour of 3 a.m., while the peak effects are waning but the essence of the experience still lingers, the returning intellect devotes its energies to understanding what has been felt. Later, when all intellectual functions have returned, the individual can attempt to apply to living that which he has understood from the experience.

When you take a mind-altering sacrament you are affecting the mental world through the physical world (i.e., a biochemical change). The experience may be demanding on the mind and body. Your mind and body should be in a condition which is harmonious with the experience. You should be well rested, relaxed and in good general health. Nutrition plays an important role in both physical and mental well-being. Balances and disbalances of certain nutriments may profoundly influence the state of consciousness. In addition to the general rules of good nutrition, which are well covered in other writings, the following suggestions are offered:

Supplementary doses of vitamin C should be taken before and after the experience. This vitamin increases the effectiveness of most drugs and is also important in removing residual toxins from the body. B-vitamin intake should be increased, many of these are antistress factors. We do not recommend the use of fractured or synthetic vitamins unless specific deficiencies are noted. The best source of antistress B-vitamin factors is liver. Kidney, soybeans and brewers' yeast are also good sources. People who exhibit schizoid tendencies or experience non-drug-induced hallucinations may do well to avoid mind alterants altogether. A person having this sort of problem may be suffering from adrenolutin poisoning connected with inadequate

Doors to the mind

Unifying Tree of Life

production of one of the body's coenzymes known as NAD (nicotinamide adenine dinucleotide). Niacin (vitamin B3) is needed by the body to produce this coenzyme. Doctors trained in orthomolecular psychiatry are having excellent results with schizophrenic patients by giving them massive doses (more than 3 grams daily) of niacin with an equal amount of vitamin C. A combination of 1 to 2 grams of B3 with B6, C and tranquilizer is often used as an antidote for LSD-induced psychosis. Caution is advised in this treatment because the vitamins in that quantity can potentiate the effects of some tranquilizers.

A commonplace practice of people all over the world with experience in the use of mind alterants is fasting or restricting of diet around the time of a ceremony. Some of the substances most commonly avoided at this time are: salt, alcohol, coffee, fat, and meat—especially pork and chicken. Many people in our own culture prefer to fast or eat very lightly before taking mind-altering sacraments. A full stomach can be distressing during the experience.

SIGNIFICANCE OF SACRAMENTS

The presence of certain useful chemical properties within various substances is Nature's indication of both our right to use these substances and our responsibility to learn to use them rightly.

The ecclesiastical definition of a sacrament is: an outward and physical manifestation of an inward and spiritual grace. In most religious and tribal beliefs this definition remains appropriate. Whether it be the Christian eucharist spiritually transubstantiated into the bod/ of Christ, the peyote of the Huichol Indians inhabited by the spirit of Elder Brother, or the sacred psilocybe mushroom reverently spoken of by its worshipers as "the Flesh of God," a sacrament is more than a means to an end. To the devout and respectful it is in itself a sacred thing because it is believed to be manifested by a divine presence.

A sacrament may take the form of a mind alterant, a nutriment, a healing agent or anything that the individual believes can be an instrument for his maintenance or betterment. If he is part of a primitive society lacking in science, he may attribute the sacrament's powers to the mere presence of a divine entity. But if he is a member of a scientifically erudite society, he can explain the substances' effectiveness in terms of alkaloids or other chemicals acting in some pharmacologically predictable manner.

If this same scientifically erudite individual chooses to recognize the existence of a Supreme Being, it is not unreasonable for him to believe that these chemicals are present in that substance by Divine Will and are therefore manifestations of Deity. If this individual also believes that the human being is capable of free will, it is natural and logical for him to assume that it is his God-given right and responsibility to exercise this gift of free will when his choices and actions do not invade the rights of any other being. This most pertinently applies to the individual's right to choose and use any sacraments which God or Nature has provided.

In the United States many substances are prohibited or restricted by law. A church cannot name these substances as its sacraments and expect Constitutional protection of its right to use them. The Constitutional guarantee of religious freedom does not allow a church to adopt any mode of behavior which has been previously established by the statutes as illegal. .

The Church of the Tree of Life has named as its sacraments all substances in the physical universe which are not presently illegal. We have faith that the Constitution of the United States will protect our right to continue to employ these sacraments. The substances described in this and other Books of Sacraments are the Major Sacraments of the Church of the Tree of Life. We most especially expect protection of our right to use these substances.

SACRAMENTS AND MAGIC

Traditional rites and ceremonies often accompany the sacramental ingestion of psychotropic plants. It is of great benefit to those using drugs as the keys to the archetypes of human consciousness to study the practices of those who have taken this path before. Rituals are used to "program" a religious awakening. Sense stimuli are chosen as cues, helping the worshiper to recognize that aspect of deity invoked and to integrate the revelation harmoniously with past and future experience. (That is, to have a good trip.) There are certain fundamental characteristics of all

Magician causes change with the Will

Archetypes of consciousness

such ceremonies that are independent of cultural differences and that provide a basis for modifying and adapting to present needs.

The High Priest, or Magician, is the "Changer" of consciousness. A Magician is anyone who attempts to cause change to occur in conformity with his Will, and who accepts the Karmic responsibility for his acts. Magicians may serve as guides for one or more other persons, or may work alone. Anyone who changes his own or someone else's consciousness with a psychoactive substance is in a very real sense assuming the role of Magician by putting Magic into practice. He should therefore familiarize himself with magical theory and the duties and privileges of his magical grade.

The Magic Circle

The Magician must find a Magic Circle. Worshipers should gather in places as free from distraction as possible. This may be in a grove of trees, on a mountaintop, in a private room, or in a cathedral. When working with sacraments it is sometimes convenient to fix the Magic Circle at the limits of the physical body itself. Then the Magician need only be master of his body (the true Temple of God) to be in control of his circle. Magic Circles should be large enough to perform the operation comfortably, but not larger than the Magician can control easily. Let the Spirit called "Practice" be your guide in this matter.

The Invocation

The premise that specific objects, drugs, odors, symbols, chants, etc. lead the mind to specific places is the basis of sympathetic magic. These specific places or archetypes of consciousness have a definite one-to-one correspondence with the spinal energy centers known in Tantric systems as chakras. Such root experiences have also been personified as the gods and goddesses of mythology. Any particular archetype differs greatly from the next, yet remains true to itself throughout time and cultural changes. The Adepts and brujos know this fact well. That is why their chants and rites are different for each type of sacrament. Each drug-bearing substance will magnify a different cosmic potency within the circle and the body and mind of the Magician. An ingested substance is a necessary element in many magical operations. Because of its physicalness it serves as a magical link with the physical plane and the physical body of the Magician. To assure one-pointedness it is good to place within the circle sense objects which are sympathetic to the Work. Then, if the mind of the Magician should wander through his senses, he will be reminded of his task by the very nature of these stimuli and will thus be brought back again to the predetermined point of concentration.

The invocation leads the mind

In theory by ingesting a substance consecrated to a given archetype the forces and "intelligences" operative in that sphere will align themselves with or come under the control of the Magician. This is assuming that the Magician is truly master of his Circle. In most cases energies generated in this way have a positive effect on the persons involved. Sometimes, however, the Magician is not psychologically prepared to handle the situation. The forces will then seem to be demonic in nature and may even attempt to take control of the Circle or the Magician himself. Some drugs are relatively harmless or seem to have only beneficial effects, while others can be very harmful to those who are not ready for such experiences, or to those who misuse the drug. These angel/demon forces are described and categorized by modern scientists who know them as alkaloids, etc., instead of as spirits. Science has made it possible for modern magicians and alchemists to be very specific in mapping and preprogramming initiatory experiences.

The mescaline-bearing cacti peyote and San Pedro both contain sets of secondary alkaloids which alter the mescaline experience. Because the secondary alkaloids in peyote vary from those in San Pedro, the effects are different and therefore the traditional ceremonies for the two sacraments are not the same. One might say that peyote spirits are different from San Pedro spirits and that each set of spirits has its own doors to open and powers to grant.

Sympathetic Correspondence

For each sacrament there are certain sense impressions that are harmonious, and others that are not. For example many commonly available incenses are often burned in magical ceremonies. Some of these are more compatible with certain operations than others. Many of these relationships have been catalogued by the Western mystery schools.

The following table based on the ancient Kabalistic Tree of Life should help in avoiding mistakes while dealing with these forces. Some major planetary and astrological attributions are also supplied for those who are familiar with that system. It is best to pick a time for your work when the planetary influences corresponding to the sacrament being used are favorable, and to avoid times that are poorly aspected. Also check aspects to your own natal chart at these times. All attributions on the same horizontal line of the table are magically sympathetic to each other, and may be used together to strengthen the vibration which attracts the desired energy to the circle.

—Frater C. A. **Order of T.O.T.**

The reading listed below will be of interest to those who wish to do further study.

Achad, Frater. *The Anatomy of the Body of God.* New York,

Weiser, 1969 Case, Paul Foster. *Tarot.* Richmond, Va., Macoy, 1947 Crowley, Aleister. *The Book of Thoth.* New York, Weiser,

1971 (second revision). Chico, Calif., OTO, 1969

Fortune, Dion. *The Mystical Qabalah.* London, Ernest Benn

Ltd., 1969

Because much attention in this book has been devoted to the magical and mystical uses of certain sacraments within various cultures we feel that a brief explanation of the practical nature of magic would be helpful to the reader. The following article was written especially for the Church of the Tree of Life by Frater C.A. of the T.O.T. Although the Order is not directly related to the Church, its beliefs and feelings about life strongly parallel our own. —Ed.

* TABLE OF SYMPATHETIC CORRESPONDENCES OF MIND-

NUMBER	ASTROLOGICAL ATTRIBUTION	DRUG	INCENSE	MAGICAL TOOL
zero	Pluto	elixir of life soma psilocybe mushroom	ambergris	crown swastika dagger fan
one	Uranus	hashish marijuana cocaine	musk	lingam inner robe wand, sceptre caduceus
two	Saturn	belladonna tobacco	myrrh	yoni outer robe bow & arrow cross
three	Neptune	drugs in general	civet	cross of suffering the wine the sacrament
four	Jupiter	opium kava	cedar	sceptre horns
five	Mars	cerebral & muscle stimulants	tobacco	sword spear scourge or chain
six	Sun	alcohol, ergot morning glory oliluique lysergic acid goldenseal	olibanum	lamen rosy cross tripod
seven	Venus	damiana	benzoin rose sandalwood	lamp furnace girdle
eight	Mercury	peyote cactus	storax	wand magical name censer
nine	Moon	San Pedro yohimbe ginseng	jasmine	perfumes sandals magic mirror
ten	Earth	corn	dittany of Crete	magic circle

* See text, page 31.

LTERING SACRAMENTS, PREPARED BY FR. C.A. OF THE T.O.T.

MAGICAL POWER	PLANT	ANIMAL	PART OF BODY	HEBREW NAME	COLOR
upreme attainment nion with God	almond in flower	God	top of head	*kether* (crown)	brilliance
ision of God face to face	amaranth	man	third eye	*chokmah* (wisdom)	white or soft blue
ision of sorrow	cypress opium poppy	woman	skeleton	*binah* (understanding)	gray
ision of self-knowledge	lotus water plants	child- savior	glandular system	*daath* (knowledge)	rainbow
ision of love	olive shamrock four-leaf clover	unicorn	viscera	*chesed* (mercy)	violet
ision of power	oak nettle	basilisk	musculature	*geburah* (strength)	red-orange
ision of harmony	acacia bay laurel	phoenix lion	heart	*tipareth* (beauty)	clear rose pink
ision of beauty triumphant	rose	lynx	throat	*netzach* (victory)	green
ision of splendor	moly peyote	jackal	arms	*hod* (splendor)	yellow
ision of the machinery of the universe	mandrake damiana San Pedro	elephant	genitals	*yesod* (foundation)	indigo
ision of the holy guardian angel	willow lily ivy	sphinx	base of spine	*malkuth* (kingdom)	black

A NUPTIAL CEREMONY

The ceremony is held out of doors in a place where one can feel close to nature. The guests are seated in a semicircle facing the bride and groom, who are seated upon cushions facing each other two or three feet apart. If they are in a place where peyote is not prohibited they may share a button, which the minister has broken for them. They meditate within each other's gaze. The minister, participants and guests also engage in meditation or contemplation.

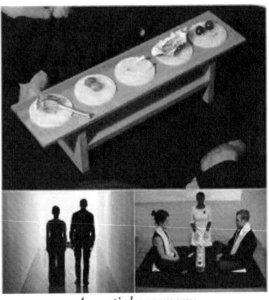

A nuptial ceremony

Positions for Wedding Ceremony

The meditation lasts about 20 minutes. In this instance the couple have some sentiments for their Christian-Judaic origins but are not bound to any orthodoxy. Therefore the minister reads an abbreviated version of Genesis 2:18-25:

And the Lord God said: "It is not good that man should be alone; I will make for him a helpmeet." And God created a woman and brought her unto the man. And the man said: "She is now bone of my bones, and flesh of my flesh." Therefore shall a man leave his father and his mother, and shall cleave unto his wife, and they shall be as one flesh. And they were both naked, the man and his wife, and they were not ashamed.

Lovers

The best man and the maid of honor pour yohimbe tea, which they present to the minister, who in turn presents it to the couple. They drink. The minister then reads a dedication to the power of lov excerpted from the Song of Songs 8:6-7:

Song of Songs

Set me as a seal upon thy heart.
For love is stronger than death,
While jealousy is cruel as the grave.
The flames of love are the fires of the Lord
Many waters cannot quench love,   *. ,*
Nor can the floods drown it;
And if one offers all of his gold for love,
Still it cannot be purchased.

The best man and maid of honor present pure yohimbine powder and the appropriate paraphernalia to the minister, who proffers it to the couple that they may inhale it as a snuff. We recommend that very small symbolic amounts be used, perhaps 5 mg per person, but the amount taken is the prerogative of the individuals. The minister asks if the couple take each other as husband and wife. They agree. The ring or pair of rings is offered and placed upon the finger. The minister pronounces them husband and wife. The couple kiss. The ceremony is completed.

Other materials suitable for reading at a wedding ceremony are the sections "On Love" and "On Marriage" from *The Prophet* by Kahlil Gibran.

The partaking of sacramental substances is a highly personal matter. No human has the right to prevent another from taking a sacrament; neither has he the right to coerce another to partake of one. One marriage partner must never insist that the other take yohimbe or any other sacrament in the ceremony.

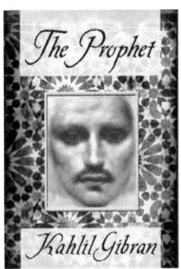

The Prophet by Kahlil Gibran

FUTURE OF FREEDOM

Most of us who have taken psychedelics have enjoyed a fascinating inner journey. Many of us have gained psychological and spiritual insights from the experience. A few of us who were not well-disposed towards these substances were confused or even shattered by the journey. The legal authorities have attempted to prevent this minority of mishaps by prohibiting the majority from using these psychocatalysts. This approach always has and always will prove worse than futile.

"Alchemists" of the twentieth century are continually discovering new mind alterants in both the natural and synthetic worlds. The authorities have placed restrictions on many of the chemicals used in synthesizing these drugs. The "alchemists" in turn have devised alternate methods of synthesis.

A few simple reactions can convert gramine, an alkaloid found in barley sprouts, into DMT. Parsley seeds, anise seeds and many other common foods are but a step or two away from being powerful psychoactive agents. It would be hopeless to attempt to control these substances through prohibition. Legislators would have to outlaw most of the natural world.

Mankind has found new doors to his mind and new keys to open them. That he will use these keys to open these doors is inevitable. As he evolves into a stronger, wiser and more independent being mankind realizes that it is his moral right to travel through the doors of his own mind.

While the lawbooks reflect an attitude that the individual and his mind are the property of society, twentieth-century man rebels and says: "I am the property of myself. My mind is my territory and the final frontier of my privacy. I am captain of my own ship."

The drug laws and other statutes controlling private behavior have not furthered society. They have only succeeded in creating crime and criminals and in alienating millions of good people. We are not children. We cannot tolerate an over-protective father figure in a judicial robe or police uniform telling us how we must conduct our private lives.

We need only two things: freedom to make our own choices and knowledge to make these choices wisely.

The Church of the Tree of Life is a way for humanity to come together during these times to voice its cry for freedom and pool its resources for knowledge. The Church serves as a unifying agent to assist humanity through the crisis of this phase of our evolution. When the crisis has passed, when rationality, harmony and freedom are restored, when the state sees itself once more as public servant rather than public master, the Church will no longer be needed. Then it will dwindle and in its place we will find only ourselves—strong, wise, benevolent and independent.

ARECA

(Areca catechu)

A sacrament for solace and stimulation during journey or labor.

Other names: *betel nut, areca nut, betel morsel, pinang, siri, supari (Hindu), ping lang (Chinese).*

Throughout most Asian countries hundreds of millions of people chew the nut from this tree of the Palm family (Palmae) for its stimulating and spirit-lifting effects. The nuts are collected by adolescent boys and girls, who spend their days among these palms harvesting and making love. These nuts are then wrapped in a betel leaf, which is the leaf of the vine *Piper betle* of the Pepper family (Piperaceae). To this is added a pinch of burnt lime (hydrated calcium oxide), some catechu gum from the Malayan acacia tree. *Acacia catechu* of Bean family (Leguminosae) and a dash of nutmeg, cardamom or turmeric for flavoring. These betel morsels are then sold on the streets and in the marketplaces. The morsel is held in the mouth and sucked on for hours like a piece of can

Areca catechu

Betel Nut

dy. In combination with saliva the lime helps to release the arecoline from the nut.

Arecoline is a volatile oil which acts as an excitant to the central nervous system. It increases respiration and decreases the work load of the heart.

Excessive arecoline from either immoderate use or from chewing unripe areca nuts which contain large quantities of the oils can cause inebriation, dizziness and diarrhea. It is also believed that excessive, long-term use of areca nuts may eventually weaken sexual potency. The regular use of betel morsels does in time stain the mouth, gums and teeth deep red. "This is harmless and held to be a point of pride among Asian betel chewers but it is considered unsightly by Western cultures.

Ayahuasca

(Banisteriopsis caapi vine)

A visionary potion.

Other names: *yagé or yajé, natem, shori (Peru),*
"liana of the soul"

Ayahuasca is a famous visionary potion invented by shamans in the Amazon jungle. Although there is no evidence to support the superstition that ayahuasca facilitates telepathy, this botanical sacrament can indeed occasion deep mystical rapture with vivid visions of archetypal significance. A moderate ayahuasca experience might last less than six hours. A stronger dose, particularly with subsequent "booster" doses, might prolong the session up to ten hours or more.

Ayahuasca is a tea brewed from the *Banisteriopsis caapi vine*, which is usually mixed with an herb containing DMT. The leaves of *Psychotria viridis*—called "chacruna" by Shipibo Indians—are the most widely used DMT source. Pure DMT is psychoactive when smoked, but it is ordinarily inactive when consumed orally. Although it has never

Banisteriopsis caapi vine

been scientifically proven, most armchair drug pundits pontificate that the harmala alkaloids in *Banisteriopsis caapi* cause MAO-inhibition that enables the DMT to become orally active. And although MAO-inhibition occurs in many parts of the body, no scientist has ever bothered to prove where in the human body the MAO-inhibition actually permits drugs such as DMT to become orally active, if indeed this is the reason (or one of the reasons) that DMT is active when consumed in ayahuasca.

Although *Banisteriopsis caapi* leaves also contain harmala alkaloids, the natives always use the wood stems, which must be pounded into mashed fibers before being stewed in water along with the leafy herbs. It is important to simmer the herbs, never letting them reach a rolling boil. If the concoction boils then the sugars will caramelize, causing an extremely bitter taste. If the mixture simmers without boiling, then it will still taste quite bitter, but will be more palatable with a sweet aftertaste. That said, some shamans do boil both during extraction and reduction, and they just live with the increased bitterness.

Indigenous South American shamans may also add tobacco and other "tertiary admixture" plants, some of which pharmacologically modify the experience and some of which have a symbolic or magical function. Some shamans add *Brugmansia* ("toé" in Shipibo), the so-called "tree Datura". Like *Datura*, these related Solanaceous species are toxic and can be fatal in larger amounts. They cause a disorienting stupor and vivid hallucinations that are far less desirable than those produced by the classic psychedelics. Shaman's who use *Brugmansia* are said to develop X-ray vision, but

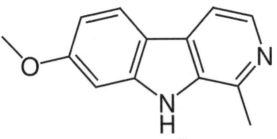

Molecular structure of harmine

Ayahuasca shamans

they do not live very long because of this plant's toxicity. Ayahuasca shamans are called *ayahuasqueros*. Sometimes, *ayahuasqueros* traveling to the United States operate a scam. They are afraid of being arrested for possessing a potion containing the illegal chemical DMT. So they add *Brugmansia* to their brew instead. When the American clients specifically ask if the *ayahuascqua* contains *Brugmansia*, the shaman will lie and insist that it does not. But the clients end up having unpleasant experiences due to being dosed with the toxic plant.

The ayahuasca vine and chacruna leaf are now cultivated in frost-free areas of the United States such as Hawaii, Florida, and Puerto Rico. Do-it-yourself *ayahuasqueros* in America should simmer their batch of herbs, pour off the liquid, then add more water for another batch. After collecting several batches of dilute tea, most of the alkaloids will have been extracted. The volume is reduced by simmering the tea till it is quite concentrated. Do not reduce the first batch and then pour subsequent batches into the pot containing the reduced first batch, because this will cause the first batch to undergo prolonged cooking that will reduce its potency. Instead, ensure that all of the batches are cooked for the same amount of

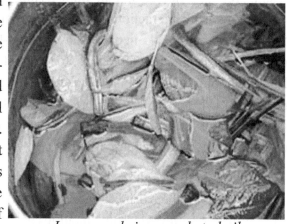
Leaves and vines ready to boil

time. The idea is to reduce the tea so that it is sufficiently concentrated so that one serving fits into a small glass. Because ayahuasca is one of the most bitter of commonly used sacramental potions, it is best to have to swallow only one small cup. However, if you try to reduce it too far then it risks caramelizing or worse yet burning. So keep a careful eye on it lest you ruin all your hard work by letting your potion burn at the last minute.

Ayahuasca can be stored in the refrigerator for long periods. However, because the DMT has a habit of floating to the top, the mixture must be thoroughly stirred before each use to avoid the risk of suffering a far stronger mind-blowing reaction than you planned.

Risks

Using ayahuasca has several potential risks. Fast for a few hours before taking the brew is needed. An empty stomach is required because vomiting may occur in novices or people having a particularly heavy experience involving the discharge of intense emotions.

People are usually advised to avoid in particular foods containing tyramine, such as aged cheese, lest a hypertensive crisis result. Yet it is not clear that *Banisteriopsis* actually produces adverse medical interactions with tyramine. However, so-called "ayahuasca analogs" — in particular "pharma-huasca" might conceivably produce fatal interactions, for example some prescription MAO-inhibitors perhaps might make DMT orally active, and also might KILL a person who ingests food containing tyramine. It is important to consult a physican about such interactions before experimenting with ayahuasca.

Thousands of people successfully consume ayahuasca every year and many of them drink it quite frequently. Although ayahuasca is ordinarily non-toxic, some fatalities have occurred. It is speculated that these deaths were due to the MAO-inhibiting effects of the harmala alkaloids in the *Banisteriopsis* having a fatal pharmacologial interaction with prescription medicines such Prozac and other anti-depressant SSRIs (strategic serotonin reuptake inhibitors). Remember, some prescription medicines stay in the system for a considerable period after one discontinues ingesting them. If in doubt, do NOT ingest any ayahuasca. Again, consult your doctor if you are in doubt about a potentially dangerous synergistic interaction. However, proper toxicology data was never obtained from the few people who died after taking ayahuasca, so nobody really knows what actually happened in those cases.

Prolonged psychological reactions can result when psychological instability persists after the pharmacological effects of the brew have worn off. And acute adverse mental reactions—bummers—can occur when somebody has paranoia or delusions during the drug effects.

Westerners taking ayahuasca in a traditional South American setting should be aware that sorcery is an integral part of the belief system of the natives conducting the rituals. The use of ayahuasca to magically cure illness is the flip side of the supposed witchcraft that natives believe originally caused the illness. Of course, the emphasis on black magic is not pronounced in the Christianized ayahuasca sects such as Santo Daime or União do Vegetal (UdV). But foreigners who go to "ayahuasca tourism" performances conducted by indigenous or mestizo curanderos should be aware

Sorcery is integral in ayahuasca rituals

that sorcery is given credence in these circles. Ayahuasca is a potent mind-altering drug that can increase suggestibility, causing the tourist to get sucked into the black magic.

Some South American shamans have high standards of morality. Other ayahuasca shamans may see absolutely no conflict-of-interest in conducting a religious ceremony one evening and then the next day seducing his clients and shoplifting whatever he can pilfer from a store in town. In truth, the entire Amazon region is infested with sleazy shamans who are preoccupied with hexing each other and fleecing their well-heeled foreign clients.

In South America, ayahuasca is regarded as legal, at least for citizens of those countries. On rare occasions, *ayahuasqueros* are still charged with sorcery rather than drug possession. Foreigners who get involved with ayahuasca might run into problems if they set themselves up as curanderos or try to transport the brew. In North America, there have been numerous court cases dealing with people arrested for importing or dispensing ayahuasca that contains DMT. After a decade-long legal battle with the DEA, a branch of the União do Vegetal church in the United States finally got a Supreme Court ruling that enabled it to reach an agreement with the DEA that allowed it to dispense ayahuasca. But this narrow ruling does not automatically protect other groups from being harassed for distributing a concoction containing the Schedule I drug DMT.

An additional pitfall is that some ayahuasca enthusiasts, as well as DMT users, fall into "proselyzation mode" where they want everybody in the world to partake of this wonderful peak experience. The problem is that not everybody is cut out to have a strong psychedelic, and also some people are likely to have prejudicial attitudes toward anybody who advocates the use of any unusual psychoactive herb. Despite drawbacks and potential hazards, ayahuasca can be rewarding and interesting.

CALAMUS

(Acorus calamus)

A sacrament for stimulation, tonic and medicinal purposes, and for alleviating fatigue.

Other names: **sweet flag, rat root, sweet cane, sweet grass, sweet myrtle, sweet rush, sweet sedge, sweet-root, cinnamon-sedge, myrtle-sedge, myrtle-flag, myrtle-grass, beewort, sweet calomel, bach (Hindu), vacha (Ayurvedic), ch'ang pu (Chinese).**

This semi-aquatic perennial of the Arum family (Araceae) is often found in marshes and borders of streams and ponds from Nova Scotia to Minnesota, southward to Florida and Texas. It also grows in Europe and Asia. It is commonly seen among cat-tail and other species of flag.

Calamus is mentioned throughout the Old Testament as a sacramental herb. It was one of the constituents of an ointment which Moses was commanded to rub on his body when approaching the Tabernacle:

Moreover the Lord spoke unto Moses, saying. Take thou also unto thee the chief spices, of flowing myrrh five hundred shekels, and of sweet cinnamon half so much, even two hundred and fifty, and of sweet calamus two hundred and fifty, and of cassia five hundred, after the shekel of the sanctuary, and of olive oil a hin. And thou shall make it a holy anointing oil, an essence compounded after the art of the perfumer; it shall be a holy anointing oil.

—Exodus 30:22-25

It is spoken of again in the Song of Songs:

A garden locked is my sister, my bride;

A closed spring, a fountain sealed.

Thy shoots are a garden of pomegranates

Laden with luscious fruit,

And the most precious spices:

Henna with spikenard plants.

Saffron, calamus and cinnamon;

With trees of frankincense, myrrh and aloes,

And a garden fountain of living waters.

Flowing streams from Lebanon.

Song of Songs 4:12-15

It has been praised in prose, poetry and pharmacopoeia throughout the ages. Walt Whitman wrote 45 ballads under the title "Calamus" in his *Leaves of Grass:*

Calamus taste

(For I must change the strain—these are not to be pensive leaves, but leaves of joy). Roots and leaves unlike any but themselves, Scents brought to men and women from the wild woods, and from the pond-side . ..

(Calamus no. 13)

Acorus Calumus Flower

For 2000 years calamus has held its place in both the Ayurvedic and Yunani systems of medicine as remedy for bronchitis, asthma, diarrhea, dysentery, dyspepsia and fevers, and to increase memory, brain power and lifespan. The Pharmacopoeia Indica recommends that a pinch of powdered calamus mixed with a spoonful of clarified butter be taken daily on an empty stomach and followed half an hour later with a dish of milk and rice to prolong lifespan and improve memory. In China calamus is used to relieve constipation and swellings.

In many cultures calamus root has been used as an aromatic stimulant and flavoring, for relief of dyspepsia, and as a tonic for feeble digestion. A common tonic recipe is: 1 oz. calamus boiled in 1 pt. water given in doses of a wine glass daily or before meals.

Sweet Flag
Acorus catamus

Nearly all Cree Indians over the age of 40 in northern Alberta chew calamus regularly as an anti-fatigue medicine. The usual dose is a piece about the diameter of a pencil by 1 or 2 inches long. This amount usually makes one feel light and pleasant like "walking one foot above the ground." They also use it for relief of toothache, headache, hangover and asthma, and for oral hygiene. Indians who use calamus are apparently healthier than those who do not; the users are not inclined towards alcoholism. Occasionally some Cree chew a piece about 10 inches long as a mind-altering sacrament. This much calamus may provoke vomiting. It is occasionally used in folk medicine as an emetic.

The essential oil of calamus contains the psychoactive substances asarone and (β-asarone. These are the non-amine precursors of TMA-2, a phenethylamine having 18 times the potency of mescaline.

The roots of sweet flag are collected in the late autumn or spring. Adhering dirt is washed from them and the less aromatic and more bitter rootlet fibers are removed. The roots are dried carefully with moderate heat. During this they lose about three-fourths of their weight, but improve in flavor. Much of the cala-mus root exported from Germany has been peeled before drying. These look attractive but lose much of their potency and aroma. The U.S. Pharmacopoeia directs that unpeeled rootstock be used. Stored calamus deteriorates with age and moisture, and is subject to attack by worms. It should be kept in a protected, cool, dry place.

Prior to flowering the sword-like leaves of sweet flag resemble those of other flags. There have been cases of poisoning in children when blue flag *(Iris versicolor)* of the Iris family (Iridaceae) was mistaken for sweet flag. One can easily tell the difference because the leaves of sweet' flag when scratched produce a fragrant aroma whereas those of blue flag do not. The roots of sweet flag have a pleasant odor and a pungent taste. The roots of blue flag have no odor and an acrid, nauseous taste.

In England during the 1930s depression calamus root was chewed as a tobacco substitute. Even today it is often chewed to break the nicotine habit. Because of experiments which indicated that oil of calamus might increase the incidence of tumors in laboratory animals, the Food and Drug Administration has considered prohibition of its use. We, at the Tree of Life Church, recommend that individuals be made aware of the facts so that they may make their own decisions.

CALEA

(Calea zacatechichi)

A sacrament for inducing prophetic visions, clarifying the senses and treating fevers.

Other names*: Mexican calea, thle-pela-kano (leaf of god), bitter grass.*

This inconspicuous shrub of the Sunflower family (Com-positae) ranges from central Mexico to Costa Rica. It has been used in Mexican folk medicine to reduce fevers, as an astringent for blood staunching, for diarrhea, and to stimulate appetite.

A medicinal dose usually consists of 10 grams of crushed, dried leaves in water or tincture 3 times daily, before meals. In larger doses it is used to clarify the mind and senses. In still larger doses it is used to induce prophetic hallucinations.

When used for the latter purpose among the Chontal Indians of Oaxaca the dried leaves are crushed and steeped in boiled water. The tea is drunk slowly. Then the Indian lies down in a

Calea zacatechichi

Calea zacatechichi

quiet place and smokes a cigarette rolled from the dried leaves. If he feels a great sense of repose and can hear his own heart and pulse beats, he has taken the right amount. If not, he takes more.

Alkaloids have not been found in calea. Its psychoactive and medicinal components are not as yet known, but are thought to reside in the bitter principle and the aromatic constituent.

CANARY ISLAND BROOM

and other brooms

(Genista canariensis)

A sacrament for relaxation and arousal of the intellect.

A shaman of the Yaqui tribe of northern Mexico prepares this sacrament of the Bean family (Leguminosae) in the following manner: He collects the blossoms and ages them in a sealed jar for ten days. Then he dries them in the sun or in low heat, and rolls them into cigarettes. 4"he smoke is inhaled and held for at least ten seconds. One cigarette or less produces relaxed, amiable feelings for about two hours. Several cigarettes produces more

Genista sp.

intense and longer-lasting effects--about five hours. During the first few hours physical relaxation is experienced. This is followed by a period of mental alertness, clarity and flexibility of the intellect, and heightened awareness of color and contrast without distortions or hallucinations. There are usually no unpleasant after-effects or hangover although there have been a few reports of mild headaches soon after smoking the flowers.

Other brooms such as Scotch broom *(Cytisus scoparius)* and Spanish broom *(Spartium junceum)* have been tested and found to be similar in effect but milder than the Canary Island broom.

The active component of the brooms is cytisine. When ingested this toxic pyridine can be dangerous. It has cardiac-stimulating properties similar to foxglove *(Digitalis)* and causes excitation followed by stupor or unconsciousness. Its effects are not so pronounced when smoked. Cytisine has been isolated from the beans and leaves of the brooms and is also found in red mescal beans *(Sophora secundiflora)*, a risky sacrament which the Plains Indians employed as a divining hallucinogen until they learned to use the much safer peyote button for this purpose.

GINSENG

(Panax schinseng)

A sacrament for restoring health, prolonging life, and many other medicinal purposes.

Other names: *divine root, root of life, man root, sang (American species, Panax, quinquefolium), redberry, five-fingers.*

T he "man-shaped" root of this plant of the Ginseng family (Araliaceae) has been reverently used for thousands of years by people in China, Korea, Japan, Southeast Asia, India and Siberia. They maintain that it prolongs life, prevents diseases and disorders, strengthens heart, nerves and glands, increases and regulates the flow of hormones, reduces susceptibility to certain poisons, aids in regaining strength after illness, increases sexual potency, improves blood circulation and aids digestion.

The production of ginseng in Korea is tightly controlled by

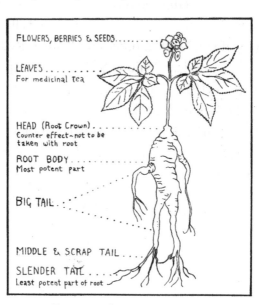

FLOWERS, BERRIES & SEEDS.........

LEAVES ....
For medicinal Tea

HEAD (Root Crown). ....
Counter effect~not to be
taken with root

ROOT BODY.............
Most potent part

BIG TAIL. .

MIDDLE & SCRAP TAIL ....

SLENDER TAIL ....
Least potent part of root

Parts and uses of Ginseng

Ginseng root

the government, but there are no restrictions against its use. Growers must sell their entire crop to the Government Off ice of Monopoly and the dried roots are handled exclusively by government-appointed export agents. Much ginseng is shipped out of Hong Kong and unscrupulous dealers often substitute cheaper materials such as American and Japanese ginseng. Many Chinese herbalists claim that Japanese ginseng may have harmful side effects.

The highest quality is Chinese Imperial, which sells for $5,000 per catty (1¹/3 lbs.). Next in order are: Korean Red Heaven 15 at $216.50/catty, American Wild at $133.30 and Japanese Red Heaven 15 at $36.60 (1971 Hong Kong Exclusive Agents prices to wholesalers and distributors). The grades of whole roots are: Heaven, Earth, Good, and Cut Roots. The grades of root tails are: Big Tail, Middle Tail, Scrap Tail and Slender Tail. The diagram shows the parts of the plant and root.

Most of the world's studies on ginseng have been carried out by Soviet scientists. According to the *Cyclopedia Dictionary of Medical Botany of the USSR* by G. S. Ogolovec (1955), ginseng contains panaxin, panaquilon, schingenin, starch, sugar, saponins, panacen (a volatile material), minerals, panaxaure (a fatty substance), vitamins B1 and B2, and the enzymes amylase and phenolase.

Most herbalists agree that ginseng should not be taken when one is sick or has a cold unless specially prescribed by an experienced herb doctor. They say that rather than being a cure it is for maintaining health and regaining health after an illness. One Korean herbalist suggests that for best results orange juice and fresh fruits should be avoided for 24 hours before and 24 hours after taking ginseng. Another herbalist teaches that ginseng should not be prepared in metal vessels, although silver vessels are sometimes used. It should be stored in crockery or glass jars.

A piece of ginseng about the thickness of a pencil and an inch long (or an equal amount of slender tails) can be moistened in the mouth and gradually chewed. A tea can be made by boiling the shaved root or the tails. Powdered ginseng can be moistened into a paste and then further combined with any liquid to make an instant tea or drink.

How Chinese Herbalists Use Ginseng

• *To stimulate blood circulation: A cup of strong ginseng tea with honey and cinnamon is taken daily.*

• To stimulate digestion: One-half teaspoon ginseng powder and 1 egg white in a glass of fresh pineapple juice is taken 3 times daily. People using this much raw egg white over a period of time are advised by us to supplement their intake of biotin, a B vitamin which is destroyed by avidin, a substance present in raw egg whites.

• For insomnia: Honey is added to an extract of equal parts chopped or powdered ginseng and orange peels.

• As a sedative: A light broth is made of ginseng and bamboo leaves.

• As a tonic to regain vigor: Boil orange peel and fresh ginger root and add powdered ginseng.

Commercial ginseng is cultivated from the seed and is usually about six years old when harvested. The American species *(P. quinquefolium)* grows wild in rich, moist soil of hardwood forests from Maine to Minnesota southward to the mountains to Northern Georgia and Arkansas. It requires partial shade and good drainage.

GOLDENSEAL

(Hydrastis canadensis)

**A medicinal sacrament for treating surface
inflammations and other disorders.**

Other names: *yellow puccoon, goldenroot, curcuma, Indian turmeric, jaundice root, yellow eye, ground raspberry,
eye balm, yellowroot.*

The root of this perennial plant of the Crowfoot family (Ra-
nunculaceae) was one of the most important medicinal materials of the American Indians. They used applications of a cold
water-goldenseal infusion as a treatment for inflamed eyes. They
also used the yellowroot juice as a skin stain, bug repellent and
cloth dye. Early settlers learned of its medicinal properties from
the Indians. The root was
chewed by Ohio and Ken-
tucky pioneers as a remedy
for sore mouth. An infu-
sion of goldenseal root in
water or spirits was used
as a bitter tonic to treat
digestive disorders and as
a stimulant. As a result of
the demand created by the
eclectic schools of medi-
cine it became an article of
commerce around 1750. In

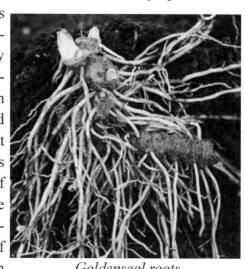

Goldenseal roots

Goldenseal Roots and Tops

1860 it was entered as an official medicinal substance in the U.S. Pharmacopoeia.

Goldenseal Roots and Tops

The plant is found growing in patches in open woods and shaded bluffs and hillsides where there is rich soil and good drainage. Its natural habitat ranges from southern New York to Minnesota and western Ontario south to Georgia and Missouri. Because so much of the demand for it was met by mercenary wild herb hunters it is not as plentiful as it once was. It is now cultivated commercially, but it is considerably more expensive than most herbs. The roots are harvested when they are two or three years old.

The roots and, to a much lesser extent, the leaves contain the well-known medicinal alkaloids hydrastine and berberine. Molecularly, these substances are related to the morphine alkaloids. In the appropriate doses they serve many medicinal functions. In larger amounts they may act as an acro-narcotic, but such quantities are dangerous because they poison the protoplasm and arrest the movement of white corpuscles.

A pinch of powdered goldenseal taken daily can stimulate the nerves and improve circulation and digestion. A teaspoon of the powder in a pint of water makes an excellent douche in cases of mild vaginal inflammation. Tincture of goldenseal and honey is effective in treating eczema, burns, cuts, bruises, boils, athlete's foot, poison oak and poison ivy. The paste is applied to the afflicted area and covered with gauze. Every three days wrappings are changed and fresh paste is applied until healing is completed.

KAVA

(Piper methysticum)

**A sacrament for welcoming special guests
and relaxing with friends and family.**

Other names: *kava-kava, ava, ava-ava,
kawa, kawa-kawa, awa, yaqona, yangona, wati,
Rauschpfeffer, keu, macropepper.*

This perennial shrub of the Pepper family (Piperaceae) grows throughout the South Pacific islands, the Hawaiian Islands, and New Guinea. It grows between six and eight feet tall and is usually found both cultivated and growing wild in cool moist highlands up to 1000 feet above sea level. Although the leaves are used medicinally it is mainly cultivated for the roots. From these a potent beverage may be prepared.

The active components in kava are six resinous alpha pyrones: kawain, dihydrokawain, methysticin, dihydromethysticin, yangonin, and dihydroyangonin. None of these is water-soluble except when emulsified. They are soluble in alcohol, oil, and other fat solvents.

People who like alcohol tend to like kava and people who do

Kava (Piper methysticum)

*Kava Wringer from Captain Cook's **Three Famous Voyages Around the World***

not don't. Most of the powdered kava in the USA seems to be inactive or nearly inactive even with emulsification. High quality CO_2 extracts on the other hand can be 70% kava lactones and a ball that is the size of a small marble will actually incapacitate most people to the point of being unable to walk or stand competently.

There are two major ethnic methods of kava preparation: the Fiji method and the Tonga method. The Fiji method is to crush the flesh inside the root bark and soak it in water for several hours until the infusion turns cloudy. This produces a pleasant beverage with excellent tonic and mild stimulant effects. The Tonga method requires that the root first be chewed before soaking in water. Saliva emulsifies the non-water-soluble pyrones so that they may be extracted into the water and assimilated into the drinker's body.

The result of this is a potent beverage which in small amounts produces a state of euphoria and in large amounts causes extreme relaxation, lethargy of lower limbs and eventual sleep. Since it depresses spinal rather than cerebral activity it does not impair mental alertness. One often has visual and auditory hallucinations. People under the influence of kava are usually cheerful and friendly.

The kava is prepared first by harvesting the rootstocks and basal stems. The bark is removed and the material is cut into pieces. Healthy adolescents with perfect teeth chew the kava before putting it into a bowl. They are instructed not to get it too soggy and not to swallow the juices. A little water—or preferably coconut juice—is poured over the kava mash and it is allowed to soak for a while.

Inside the ceremonial house the kava wringer sits behind the kava bowl. He is bare-chested and wears no ornaments. On his right stands the water pourer. On his left stands the cup bearer. Outside the house to the right rear of the wringer stands the strainer cleaner. More water or coconut juice is poured over the kava. The wringer covers the kava at the bottom of the bowl with a strainer made of hibiscus fibers. Pressing down on the strainer with the heels of his hands and his fingers he draws it toward him, pulling much of the kava with it. Full of kava pulp, the strainer is lifted above the bowl. It is wrung three times only. Each time the clenched hands are bent forward so that the liquid will not run down the arms. The wringer then passes the strainer under his right knee with his left hand and flips it to the man outside, who catches it and cleans it by snapping it several times. Then he throws it back to the wringer, who catches it with his right hand and repeats the process. This is continued until there are no more kava particles in the bottom of the bowl. The wringer wipes the rim of the bowl. He cleans the strainer himself by snapping it, then rolls it into a ball, submerges it in the kava and raises it above the bowl with both hands allowing the liquid to stream back into the bowl. This permits the chiefs to see the color of the kava and hear its sound splashing in

Kava Root

the bowl. By the sight and sound they can determine if more water should be added.

During the preparation and ceremony strict silence is observed. In former times women and children were excluded from the ceremony. This restriction, especially as regards women, has relaxed more recently. Smoking is not permitted.

When the kava is almost ready the talking chief begins the liturgy in which he tells of the mythical origins of kava. This may include the story of the birth of Tagaloa Ui, the first Samoan chieftain—fathered by the sun—and the famous kava ceremony held for him in the house of Pava; how he cut Pava's son in halves for being noisy and later returned him to life by pouring kava upon his body, clapping his hands and saying *"Soifua"* (life). Or the talking chief may tell of the two sons of Tagaloa who found a piece of wood while swimming in the deep ocean, divided it and floated upon the pieces, each in a different direction. One returned to Fitiuta where kava was grown, while the other floated to Western'Samoa where kava was unknown. He placed the piece of wood in the ground and it grew into kava to supply the island. These legends are the basis of many parts of the ceremony.

Kava Drink

Kava Ceremony

The recounting of the legend is completed at the same moment that the last fibers are removed from the kava. If the color and sound of the kava are satisfactory, the chiefs clap their hands several times. The kava is then put into coconut cups and served, usually in an order with the highest chief first. The cup bearer holds the cup at waist level with thumbs and index fingers encircling the outside of the cup. Pausing at the center of the room he lifts it to his forehead and walks toward the chief. He stops four feet in front of the chief, lets the cup rest in his right palm and lowers his right hand with his left. He places his left hand behind his back while serving the cup to the chief at chest level and then returns to the center of the house until the chief has drunk. The chief receives the cup with two hands, pours a little kava onto the floor mat and says: *"Ia fa'atasi le Atua ma i tatou i lenei aso"* (May God be with us today). He raises his cup and says *"Soifua"* (life) and the other chiefs respond by saying *"Manuia"* (blessings). If he says *"Manuia"* the others say *"Soifua."* He drinks his kava in one gulp. The others are then served. They say nothing, out simply receive the cup and drink in one gulp. The kava is stirred before each cup is poured. Those who do not care for the taste of kava may raise the cup in salutation and return it to the Dearer, or merely tap the bottom of the cup. If one accepts the kava, but does not finish it, the remainder must be discarded before returning the cup. When all have drunk and and handed or tossed their empty cups back to the server, the announcer (talking chief) says: *"Ua moto le alofi. Ale le fau ma le ipu e tautau."* ("The ceremony is completed. The bowl will hang with the strainer and cup.") Light, delectable morsels of food are then served.

On many islands the kava is no longer premasticated, but simply steeped. If the former method is used, its effects come on in about thirty minutes. It acts at first as a stimulant, during which time there may be singing, talking and dancing. After another thirty minutes its sedative influences are felt and guests may sit about or lie about relaxing or even dozing.

The taste of kava is somewhat pungent, but not bitter. It has a slightly soapy flavor and a cinnamon-like aroma.

It is not necessary to prechew the root to gain the full psychotropic effect. The root may be ground finely (or the dried root is sometimes available from herb suppliers in powdered form) and each ounce of dried material mixed with 10 ounces of water, 2 tablespoons of coconut (or olive) oil and a tablespoon of lecithin (from health food stores). These are blended in an electric blender until the beverage attains a milky appearance. Each ounce of dried kava serves 2-4 persons.

Another method which has been used is to extract the resins into hot isopropyl alcohol, strain, and evaporate the solvent using a heated water bath and vacuum suction, and redissolve the resins in just enough drinking alcohol. Alcohol acts as a vehicle to swiftly assimilate the pyrones into the system, and also potentiates their effects. Therefore we recommend that a person take very small amounts when employing this method.

Kava use in the islands is ancient. Botanists with Captain Cook's expeditions first brought it to the attention of European man. Christian missionaries outlawed it on some islands and destroyed many plantations. It was soon replaced by alcohol. There are no longer any laws against its use either in the islands or in the United States.

Kava Extract

It is generally regarded as non-toxic, but if used immoderately it can have certain undesirable side effects: Continual chewing eventually destroys tooth enamel, constant and excessive use of the fresh root with the premasticated method (or the combination with alcoholic spirits described above) can become habit-forming and after several months result in yellowing of the skin, bloodshot and weak eyes, emaciation, diarrhea, rashes, and scaly, ulcerous skin. These symptoms do not usually appear except after long, constant and excessive use of the fresh, premasticated root or the alcohol solution When kava drinking is stopped or cut down they disappear in a week or two, especially if diet is adequate. Remember, however, that symptoms are outward manifestations of long-advancing inward disruption. Be sparing in the use of all sacraments which produce undesirable effects when used excessively. This way you will gain greater benefits from these substances. Do not wait for symptoms to appear before limiting your use of these sacraments, and if they do appear, do not begin usage again as soon as they are gone. Give your entire body time, nutrition, pure water, fresh air, rest, healthful exercise and possibly a short fast to detoxify and readjust.

Many alcoholics in the islands have cured themselves of this addiction by substituting kava until they were well and then stopping the kava, which is not nearly as addicting. Kava or its extracted pyrones have been used with some success in the treatment of grand mal epilepsy and to relax (but not cure) schizophrenics. In the islands kava leaves are often applied to cuts and bruises to prevent infection and promote healing. There is evidence that kawain and possibly other kava pyrones have antibacterial activity against gonococcus and coli bacilli. We strongly recommend, however, that no one attempt self-treatment of venereal diseases. Kawain also has surface anesthetic properties similar to cocaine alkaloids.

NUTMEG

(Myristica fragrans)

**A sacrament for flavoring and for improving
digestion, and a last-resort mind alterant.**

Other names*: noz muscada, notemuge, musk nut, mace,
mada shaunda ("narcotic fruit"—ancient Hindu), jaiphal
(Hindu), jou tou k'ou (Chinese).*

The seed of this dioecious tropical evergreen tree of the Nutmeg family (Myristicaceae) is the nutmeg, whereas the fibrous
seed covering (aril) is mace. It is native to the East Indies, particularly the Bandas and Moluccas, but now it is also cultivated in the
West Indies. Nutmeg from the East Indies is more potent in flavor
and pharmacological activity than that from the West Indies.

Nutmeg Tree

Nutmeg

This spice was first imported by Arabian traders during the first centuries A.D., then by the Portuguese in 1512, by the Dutch at the beginning of the seventeenth century and later by the English and French.   - .

Nutmeg is mentioned in the Ayurvedic scriptures (the ancient Hindu books of medicine) and still remains in the Hindu Pharmacopoeia as a treatment for fever, asthma and heart disease. Arabian physicians from the seventh century A.D. used it for digestive disorders, kidney disease and lymphatic ailments. Yemenite men still consume nutmegs to in crease and maintain their sexual vigor. It is employed in Malayan medicine as an analgesic, sedative, and treatment for madness. Medieval European physicians learned of nutmeg's uses from their Arabian colleagues. It was semisuperstitiously employed as an abortifacient and emmenagogue bv late nineteenth centurv women. In 1829 the famed physiologist J. E. Purkinje recorded his personal psvchedelic experiences with nutmeg. In India it is still often mixed with tobacco snuff and added to betel morsels for flavor and effect. In the United States it became fairly popular as a marijuana substitute among bohemians, jazz musicians, and prisoners. In his autobiography Malcolm X described his prison experiences with nutmeg. He said that it "had the kick of three or four reefers."

The usual prison dose is a matchbox of ground nutmeg— about 20 grams. This amount can cause some very severe psychological and physiological effects. These effects may vary somewhat with the individual, the dose and the potency of the material. Some people enjoy it, but most see it as a rather grueling experience. Many find it difficult to swallow the required dose. Some suffer nausea during the first 45 minutes. After that silly feelings and giggling often occur. This is soon followed by dryness of the mouth and throat, flushing of the skin and reddening of the eyes. Occasionally a person will feel agitated and hyperactive, but more often he will feel heavy, intoxicated and unable to do anything but lie down. Motor functions may be confounded and speech incoherent. He may become overly conscious of his heart beat and become concerned about the seeming gaps between beats. Later he may enter a stuporous euphoric state in which he experiences profound peace of mind and dreamy visions. If he is able to move about he will usually feel like everything is in slow motion. If he is able to engage in any sexual activity he may find it especially pleasurable. Orgasm may seem to last for an hour. A person under the spell of nutmeg is likely to find himself unable actually to sleep, but also incapable of being really awake. Sleepless stupor is the most apt description of nutmeg narcosis. This condition may last

Nutmeg Grinder

for 12 hours followed by 24 hours of drowsiness during which he may sleep a lot.

The after-effects are usually quite unpleasant: aching of the bones and muscles, soreness and aching of the eyes, running nose, tiredness, depression and possible headaches. One of the best things that can be said about nutmeg intoxication is that it is too unpleasant to be addicting.

Scientists have not as yet fully determined which of the components of nutmeg is responsible for its effects. Although some physical pharmacological activity has been noted in the nonvolatile portions, the main activity apparently resides in the volatile essential oil, which comprises 5 to 15% of the nutmeg's weight. The essential oil from 20 grams of dried nutmeg contains about 200 mg. myristicin, 70 mg. elemicin, 40 mg. safrole, and 20 mg. methyleugenol, plus several related oils in smaller amounts, and some terpenes. Safrole, which is the main component of sassafras oil, is the non-amine form of the psychedelic MDA, and is known to have psychopharmacological activity. The amount present in nutmeg, however, is by itself insufficient to account for the effects described above. It has been suggested that safrole and related non-amines may convert to their amine forms (MDA, TMA etc.) in the body by reacting with ammonia.

It is now generally agreed that the myristicin fraction is responsible for the psychotropic effects of nutmeg. It is not certain what role elemicin plays because it has been impossible to separate myristicin and elemicin by fractional distillation. There is much evidence that myristicin, elemicin, safrole and several other aromatic fractions combine synergistically to produce the psychotomimetic and narcotic effects and that the terpenes enhance their absorption into the system. Myristicin is a methylenedioxy-substituted compound similar in structure to mescaline but lacking the terminal nitrogen on the side chain. It is the non-amine precursor of MMDA--a psychoactive substance related to mescaline but with three times its potency.

There are several species of *Virola*—also of the Myristicace-ae—the resins of which are employed as hallucinogenic snuffs by South American natives. Although they also contain myristicin, the main active components are a series of tryptamine derivatives. There are no reports of tryptamines in nutmeg.

The essential oils of nutmeg are usually obtained through steam distillation. Mace, which is somewhat less sweet than nutmeg, contains about the same quantities and qualities of active substances. The leaf of the nutmeg tree contains about 1.5% essential oils.

Ground nutmeg and mace lose their essential oils rather quickly. For this reason 10 grams (two seeds) are usually taken to equal 20 grams of the ground material. We have heard reports of hallucinogenic experiences from 5 grams with a minimum of unpleasant side effects and hangover. If any individuals choose to employ nutmeg as a sacrament we recommend that 5 grams or less be used and that subsequent increases be approached gradually and cautiously.

Before taking large doses of nutmeg one should have a bowel movement and relieve the bladder. Nutmeg often makes urination difficult and has constipating effects similar to paregoric and the opiates. Fruit juices should be on hand to relieve the dry mouth condition described earlier. Some people have no desire for food during a nutmeg experience; others develop a craving for sweets.

Nutmeg oils tend to increase fat deposits on the liver. Safrole has been proven to be carcinogenic (tumor-inducing) and hepato-toxic (toxic to the liver). Persons with personal or family histories of cancer, tumors or liver disorders are advised not to use quantities of nutmeg. We strongly advise against the use of any mind-altering sacrament while operating a motor vehicle or engaging in any potentially dangerous task which demands the best from our motor reflexes. We are most emphatic about this in the case of nutmeg.

OLOLIUQUI
Morning Glory (Bindweed) Family
(Rivea corymbosa)

A sacrament for determining the cause of maladies, for finding lost or stolen items, and to consult depths of wisdom which are otherwise difficult to reach.

Other names: *(a) Rivea corymbosa (ololiuqui): semilla de la Virgen, Coaxihuitl (Aztec for snake plant), coatl xoxoulique (Aztec for green serpent), piule, la senorita, bador, Turbina corymbosa, Ipomoea sidaefolia, choisy; (b) Ipomoea violacea: tlitlitzen, badoh negro, badungas, badoh, la'aja shnash, Mexican morning glory.*

O loliuqui is the ancient Nahuatl name for the roundish seeds of *Rivea corymbosa.* It means "round things." The plant belongs to the Bindweed family (Convolvulaceae). Also in this family, having nearly the same psychoactive chemistry and employed similarly by various Indian peoples of Mexico, is badoh negro, the Zapotec name for the seeds of a Mexican variety of morning glory *(Ipomoea violacea),* also of the Bindweed family. In many villages the black badoh negro seeds are referred to as "macho"—male—and are used by the men, while the lighter-colored *Rivea* seeds are called "hembra"— female—and are used by the women.

Some species of *Argyreia, Convolvulus* and *Stictocardia* (also Bindweed family) contain the same psychoactive alkaloids. Most well-known among these are the seeds of the baby Hawaiian wood rose *(Argyreia nervosa)*. It and these others may be regarded as sacramental equivalents of the *Ipomoea* and *Rivea* species.

Ipomoea violacea is found at various elevations throughout Mexico. *Rivea corymbosa* grows abundantly in the mountains of Southern Mexico. These seeds are employed

Morning Glory (Ipomoea violacea)

by many tribes of Oaxaca including Zapotecs, Mazatecs, Mixtecs and China-tecs. The procedure for use is somewhat influenced by Catholicism and is more or less as follows:

The person planning to take the sacrament must first solemnly commit himself to do so. He must go out and cut branches bear-

Morning Glory is an aggressive vine.

Morning Glory Bud

ing the seeds. A vow to the Virgin is made. If the ritual is for diagnosis and healing, the sick person must seek out a child between seven and eight years old. A girl for a man; a boy for a woman. The child is bathed and dressed in clean clothes. The ritual takes place on a Friday at 8 or 9 p.m. Only the child, the patient and the curandero are present. There must be no noise. *Rivea* seeds are measured out by the curandero either as a thimbleful, a cup of the hand measure, or in multiples of seven—that is, 7, 14, or 21 seeds. Because they are smaller, a larger number of *Ipomoea* seeds are used. Among some tribes 13 *Rivea* seeds are used, this being a magical number as well as representing Jesus and the twelve apostles.

The curandero begins grinding the seeds on a metate (a stone grinding board) while praying that the cause and cure of the ailment be revealed. The thoroughly ground seeds are soaked in a little water for a short while. The liquid is then strained through a clean cloth and wrung by hand. When giving the drink to the patient, the curandero says three Pater Nosters and three Ave Marias. The child carries the bowl and a cense? of burning copal incense. The patient sits up, drinks and lies down. They wait for the drink to take effect. If the patient's condition improves, he stays in bed. If not, he gets up, lies before the household altar for a while, then gets up and returns to bed. No one talks until the next day, but if the session has been successful, the cause of illness and the cure are intuitively revealed to either the patient, the child or the curandero. Some Indians say that when seeking a cure or a lost or stolen object "the little people" come and whisper the secret in the ears of the person who has taken the seeds. If there is not total silence their whispers cannot be heard. Many people find noise or wordy conversation bothersome when they are within the sphere of sacraments of this group. Most curanderos insist that a person taking these sacraments follow the same rules of abstinence required for the use of psilocybe mushrooms, i.e., avoiding salt, fat, chicken, pork, alcohol and sexual relations for four days before and four days afterwards.

The most psychopharmacologically active component of this group of sacraments is Lysergic acid amide. It has about one-tenth the microgram potency of LSD. It is present in the form of a salt and is therefore soluble in water, but not in ether or alcohol unless it is first hydrolyzed with a 10% ammonium hydroxide solution. This alkaloid is also present in the leaves and stems, but in lesser concentrations than in the seeds. Turbicoryn, a crystalline glucoside with antitension and CNS-stimulating properties, has been found in the seeds of *Rivea corymbosa*. All of this group of sacraments also contain several other lysergic acid derivatives including ergine, iso-ergine, chanoclavine and elymoclavine. *R. corymbosa* also contains lysergol, while I.*violacea* instead contains ergometrine, a strong hemostatic and uterotonic.

Varieties of *Ipomoea violacea* in the United States which contain d-lysergic acid amide are: Heavenly Blue, Pearly Gates, Flying Saucers, Wedding Bells, Blue Star and Summer Skies.

The effect of these alkaloids in combination is similar to LSD and other hallucinogens, but more tranquil. Some people experience nausea during the first hour. Large doses are not recommended. After the major effects have worn off one usually feels very soft and relaxed.

Many people—scientists included—have said that they found no hallucinogenic effect from these seeds. It was later learned that in almost all of these instances the seeds had been swallowed whole or scarcely chewed. The seeds must be thoroughly ground or chewed to a pulp and mixed with some water to make the alkaloids available for assimilation. Because of their hardness one should grind rather than chew *Rivea* seeds.

It is not advisable for people with a history of hepatitis, jaundice, or other serious liver disease to take lysergic acid amides. Because several of the alkaloids in this family of sacraments have powerful uterus-stimulating properties we recommend that they not be taken by pregnant women.

The dose of baby Hawaiian wood rose seeds commonly employed by members of the psychedelic subculture is 4-8 seeds. Each round pod contains four seeds. The standard procedure is to scrape or singe the white layer from the seed coat before grinding. This layer is believed to contain a strychnine-like alkaloid which may cause undesirable symptoms. Many people suffer nausea during the first hour of a wood rose experience. If the body wishes to vomit, it should be allowed to do so. We recommend starting with no more than two seeds.

PEYOTE

(Lophophora williamsii)

A sacrament for aiding in contemplation of problems, liberating energies, purifying the mind and body, and solemnizing weddings.

Other names: *peyotl (Aztec), hikuri wanami (Huichol), challote (parts of Texas), pellote, mescal button, pioni-yo, pejori (Opata), beyo (Otomi), peyori (Pima), walena (Taos), mescalito (Yaqui), hos (Mescalero Apache), kama-ba (Tepehuánes), watara (Cora), hikuli (Tarahumare).*

Some tribes including the Huichol recognize two distinct forms of peyote: The large, more potent and more bitter buttons are called tzinouritehua-hiku-ri, which means "peyote of the gods." The smaller buttons (probably an earlier age-phase of the other) are called rhaitou-muanitari-hikuri, "peyote of the goddesses." They are more palatable than the larger buttons and are said to be milder. However, we have found them often to be surprisingly potent.

Peyote Cluster
(Lophophora williamsii)

This button-like cactus grows wild in Central Mexico and Southern Texas. It is sometimes found in open, sunlit places, but usually grows in mesquite or creosote thickets, or in the shade of larger desert plants such as opuntia, euphorbia and yucca. The buttons are dark bluish-green and grow close to the ground; therefore they may be difficult to find.

Peyote includes at least fifteen B-phenethylamine and simple isoquinoline alkaloids including mescaline (a hallucinogen), anhalonine (a reflex excitant), pelotine (a convulsant), lophophorine (respiratory stimulant), anhalonidine, anhalamine, N-methylmescaline, N-acetylmescaline, and O-methylanhalonidine. Because the peyote and mescaline experiences differ qualitatively from each other in some ways it is apparent that the other alkaloids combine synergistically with mescaline to produce a unique effect. The mescaline yield is about 6% by weight of the dried button.

Peyote Rituals

The peyote rituals of the Huichol Indians of Central Mexico still closely resemble pre-columbian practices. Christian figures, symbols and concepts have not entered the ceremony. When these people desire peyote a pilgrimage or hunt is arranged, usually during winter. Before the hunt a ceremony is held in which the peyote seekers (peyoteros) must publicly acknowledge all sexual trans-

Huichol beaded art use in Peyote Ritual

gressions. Spouses and lovers are not permitted to display or entertain negative feelings such as jealousy, anger or hurt. A knot is tied in a cord for each incident mentioned. The purpose

of this ceremony is to liberate the peyotero from his adulthood so that he may be as a child once more and thus be allowed entrance to the "magical peyote country."

Journeying

A shaman leads the journey. While the tepu drum is sounded gourds are shaken by children who are attached as a team to a string, and whom the shaman has symbolistically transformed into hummingbirds so that they may lead the way to the peyote. The shaman chants:

> *Behold, you hummingbirds;*
> *Indeed, we go where peyoteros have gone*
> *On ancient peyote pilgrimages.*
> *Who knows if we will arrive*
> *For the journey is dangerous.*
> *One must fly high to pass over the wind.*
> *Lightly as air.*
> *We will camp beneath the highest trees.*
> *Elder Brother guides them. He tells them where to fly*
> *That they may enter safely*
> *Like a string of beads they rise. How beautiful our pil-*
> *grimage. So speaks Elder Brother.*

Elder Brother, Kauyumarie (Deer Tail), is the overspirit of all deer species. To the Huichol deer, peyote and maize are unified in the same spiritual complex.

Preparing peyote for ceremony

The arduous journey may take several weeks each way. Participants must abstain from sex, salt, and chile. Dried tortillas are the only nourishment allowed. Very little water is taken. At one point of the journey known as the Gateway of Clashing Clouds there is said to be great danger (mystical and spiritual rather than physical). Novice pilgrims are blindfolded to protect them from this danger and from the blinding brilliance of the Sacred Peyote Land. After entrance to this "magical land" each person is given a cup of water to drink. The shaman removes the blindfolds and pours water over the novices' heads.

When in their search they find the first buttons the shaman shoots at these with arrows as though they were the deer. Prayers are offered to Elder Brother asking him not to be angry for killing him. The buttons are cut above the ground leaving the roots intact. The latter can now regenerate new plants. It is wasteful to remove the roots since they contain no active alkaloids. Upon

Tsuwiri (A. retusus)

picking a button it is touched to the forehead, face, throat and heart. Then it is eaten or added to the collection. They take no more than is needed. Some peyote gifts are exchanged.

After all have had a taste of peyote they sit on the ground in a circle about a creosote bush

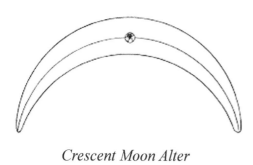

Crescent Moon Alter

or other material gathered for making a fire. Small sacrificial gifts are placed upon the kindling material. The shaman touches these gifts with his ceremonial arrow. Then he sets fire to a small wool painting which he has prepared by laying lengths of colored wool yarn upon the wax-coated surface of a flat piece of wood in spirals to form symbolic pictures. This in turn is used to ignite the bush and the offerings. A gourd filled with peyote is passed around and all partake till it is empty. The shaman may go about the circle touching the forehead, face, throat and heart of each person with a button before placing it like a eucharist in the mouth.

While waiting for the effects of the peyote to take place music is made with guitar or fiddle. Some sing or dance around the fire. Later, instruments are put aside. Participants sit about silently communing with the fire and listening to what peyote teaches. Each person receives a new name, which the Huichol say rises out of the fire in colored ribbons. Some may place about themselves a circle of candles as protection against sorcerers and evil spirits while the soul journeys from the body. The details of one's peyote experience are private and are not usually discussed with others.

Preparing the
Crescent Moon Alter

Peyote Ceremony

On the following day they bid farewell to the sacred country and implore the great spirits never to leave. The Huichol depart, taking with them some peyote for those at home.

Upon returning from the journey all gather round a fire. The knotted cord of sexual transgressions is passed around the circle, once counterclockwise behind them and once clockwise in front of them. This symbolizes transformation. Each person undoes his own knots and the cord is sacrificed to Tatewari (Grandfather Fire).

The Huichol and other peyote-oriented tribes frequently consume large quantities of peyote—a dozen buttons or more. Peyote fans in our own culture usually find three to six buttons more than enough. Many people find one button or even a piece of one

Epithelantha micromeris

very stimulating. If a member of the Church of the Tree of Life wishes to employ peyote as a sacrament we recommend that he use the smallest quantity, at least in the beginning, until he has found the correct amount for himself by gradual increase.

How Peyote Is Used

Peyote has a very bitter taste. People have tried many ways to disguise this. They have boiled it to a tea, reduced it to a tar, combined it with mint and other pleasant herbs and flavors, but the bitterness is still there. The Indians say that if one is of a pure heart he will not taste the bitterness. We find that by simply placing the button in the mouth and slowly chewing it as it mingles with saliva a person can let his meditations enter the heart

Dolichothele longimamma

Solisia pectinata

of the bitterness with understanding and appreciation. Then the mind can go beyond the bitterness and one can eat as much as he desires. A little grapefruit juice can be taken immediately afterwards to wash away the taste. Before eating peyote the tufts of hair should be removed.

Within a half hour after eating peyote the first effects are felt. At this point some may experience nausea. If one feels the need to vomit this urge should not be resisted. By eating the buttons slowly during an hour's time the system is not so shocked by the alkaloids and little if any nausea is felt. Many find that the grapefruit juice also counteracts the nausea.

Small amounts of peyote are used by many Indians to combat hunger, thirst and exhaustion. A person who has eaten peyote does not usually desire food for many hours. For this reason obese people have sometimes used the cactus as a reducing aid. Thin or undernourished people are advised not to take peyote too often.

The Huichol rub the juices of fresh peyote on wounds to heal them and to prevent infection. The chewed juices from dried peyote may also be used. Researchers at the University of Arizona have isolated from the cactus a water-soluble crystalline compound with antibiotic activity against many bacteria including some penicillin-resistant staphylococci.

Sunami *(Ariocarpus fissuratus)*

Donana
(Coryphantha macromerts)

Other Peyote Cacti

The Tarehumares employ as peyote many cacti other than *Lophophora.* These include: mulato *(Epitheliantha micromeris),* which is used to make the eyes large and clear to see sorcerers, to prolong life and to give speed to runners; rosa-para, said by botanists to be a later vegetative stage of mulato and sometimes listed as *MammMaria micromeris;* sunami *(Ariocarpus fissuratus)*— rare, but said to be more potent than peyote and employed in the same way or made into an intoxicating drink; tsuwiri *(Ariocarpus retusus),* which the Huichols call "false peyote" and regard as dangerous because it causes "bad trips"; cawe *(Pachycereuspecten-aboriginum),* fairly rare, but sometimes used as a narcotic.

Obregonia denegrii

Pelecyphora aselliformis flower

Other Peyote Cacti

A. kotschoubeyanus

Coryphantha runyouii

A. myriostigma

A. capricorne

Aztekium ritterii

Astrophytum asterias

Other species of cactus sometimes used are: *Ariocarpus kotschoubeanus, Astrophytum asterias, A. capricorne, A. myriostigma, Aztekium ritterii, Dolichothele longimamma, Obregonia denegrii, Pelecyphora aselliformis,* and *Solicia pectinata.* Mescaline and related alkaloids have been found in many of these. It is possible to use these cacti as sacraments in states where *Lophophora williamsii* is forbidden.

Doñana *(Coryphantha macromeris)* and *C. runyonii* contain macromerine, which is chemically related to mescaline but 1/5 its potency. There are no statutes governing these cacti.

PEYOTE RELIGION IN THE UNITED STATES

During the past few centuries peyote practices have spread northward through the U.S.A. and Canada among many Plains Indian tribes including Navaho, Sioux, Comanche and Kiowa. Between 1880 and 1885 the ceremony was standardized. By 1920 the practices of most tribes were universally consistent with only minor variations. Today these intertribal practices are organized legally as the Native American Church. This church preaches brotherly love, solid ethical ceonepts, and abstention from alcohol.

NAVAHO PEYOTE RITUAL

The ritual is held either for celebrating an event or to help someone rid himself of a physical, mental or emotional ailment. Participants usually fast on the day of the ritual, especially avoiding salt. The meeting is held on a Saturday evening in a tepee, hogan or round house with appropriate ventilation in the roof to accommodate a fire.

The four required officiators of the ceremony are Road Man, Cedar Man, Fire Man and Drum Man. Road Man is not a shaman, but rather an experienced administrator of authority who .keeps the meeting "on the road." He sits still through most of the ceremony. Humility and clarity are his talents. Cedar Man has a task of blessing and purifying the meeting with cedar smoke. Often he acts as spokesman for Road Man. Great love is the talent most required of him. Fire Man represents strength and movement. He tends the door and the fire and keeps the floor clean. When he is not busy with his many tasks he sits opposite Road Man, their gazes locked in communication. Drum Man is the heartbeat of the meeting.

Road Man brings the required artifacts: a staff, a drum, a rattle, an eagle-bone whistle, two feather fans, a bunch of sage, tobacco, rolling papers and peyote.

At 8 p.m. Road Man blows his whistle four times, once in each direction. Fire Man stands by the door to greet the people as they enter, moving clockwise about the room. They take their places seated with legs drawn up. Everything in the meeting house is ar-

ranged as in the diagram above Cedar Man sprinkles powdered cedar needles on the fire embers and fans smoke at Road Man. Road
Man purifies the peyote and artifacts with four sweeps of each
through the smoke. Drum Man does the same with the drum. Road
Man places a small bunch of sage upon the altar and on top of this
he places a large, perfectly formed peyote button. This is known as
"Chief Peyote" or "Father Peyote." He passes a sage branch clockwise around the room. Each person takes a piece and rubs it all
over himself for purification. Tobacco is passed around and each
person rolls a cigarette, which Fire Man lights with an ember. All

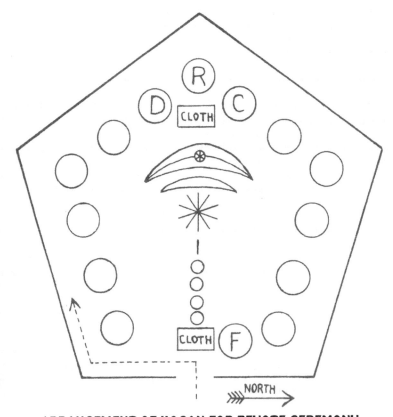

ARRANGEMENT OF HOGAN FOR PEYOTE CEREMONY
From top: Road Man, Drum Man, Cedar Man, altar cloth,
crescent altar with Chief Peyote, crescent ember bed, fire,
smoke stick, bowls of water, corn, fruit and meat, entrance cloth,
Fire Man, entrance. Participants seated round.

smoke, blowing the fumes toward the altar, the earth, the others and themselves. Fire Man places finished butts in the ember pile. Road Man says a prayer and announces the purpose of the meeting. Peyote is passed around and the participants chew it while praying silently and focusing on the altar. Road Man sings four songs. These

Indians often use Peote in religious ceremonies

are not necessarily in any known language, but may be taught to him by peyote. The drum and rattle are passed around and participants may sound them for a while or simply touch them. Peyote is passed around three or four times. One may take as little or as much as he pleases. If one becomes nauseous it is correct etiquette to vomit, for this is ridding oneself of evil. A can is provided for this. Disposal and cleaning are the tasks of Fire Man.

At midnight Road Man takes up the staff and sings. Fire Man cleans around the fire and goes outside to fetch a pail of water. Cedar Man blesses it with smoke. Fire Man kneels with a cigarette and prays, contemplating the meaning of water to life. The pail and a cup are passed to the left. All drink some. Drum Man wets his drum. Road Man waters "Chief Peyote," the staff and the rattle before drinking his share. Those who wish to be excused for a few minutes may leave the room. If anyone had a need to leave the room at any other time he would have had to indicate so with a gesture to the Road Man and get his permission, and walk behind the others so as not to step between them and the fire.

After the midnight break all are brought back to the mood — first by Cedar Man who wafts smoke at the members and then by

Road Man or Cedar Man who reminds all of the purpose of the meeting. Tobacco is smoked again. All pray silently for what they seek. The staff is passed around. During the entire ceremony no one may speak unless he holds the staff. Now each person has the chance to say what is in his heart. He may make confessions and ask forgiveness and understanding from his brothers or speak of his needs and deepest feelings. A woman rarely takes the staff to speak. It is not that she has lesser rights than man. The Indians believe that woman is intuitive and "knows"; therefore she "speaks" less often than man.

If any healing is to be done it takes place now. Road Man burns his cigarette in the fire, fans cedar smoke at the patient, gives him more peyote and fans him again.

At 3 a.m. Road Man indicates that it is that time. Prior to this participants concentrated on feeling, and let peyote show them new things. Now thoughts are turned to understanding with the mind what peyote has taught the spirit.

At dawn a fifth officiator—Earth Woman--becomes involved in the ceremony. She brings water and with Road Man and Drum Man she sings the Morning Water Song. Then she serves a light, token breakfast of water, corn, fruit and boneless meat—in that order (see placement in diagram). It is blessed by Cedar Man while Earth Woman smokes a cigarette and Road Man sings a final song. Each person takes only a morsel of food. The sage and "Chief Peyote" are removed from the altar. The ceremony is ended. All relax inside or outside. They talk and laugh. At noon a large feast is served.

PEYOTE AND THE LAW

The federal prohibition of mescaline under Schedule I (C) will certainly apply to the consumption of any cacti which contain this alkaloid. These will even include all mescaline-containing species mentioned in this book if they are being consumed. Simple possession of most of them is still legal so long as there is not suspicion or indication of actual use or preparation for use. Peyote is illegal in all 50 states based on federal law. The omission of a possession prohibition in the laws of any state or the lack of laws specifically governing peyote (*L. williamsii*) is superseded by the federal statutes that once possessed anexemption for traditional users until a couple of decades ago.

Curiously federal courts have decided that members of the Native American Church (NAC) may be denied the use peyote in their ceremonies at the state level without violating their Constitutional guarantees of religious freedom so long as the prohibitions are being uniformly applied to all people. Congress responded by granting all federally recognized tribes the right to consume peyote—whether its use had any traditional historical basis in their culture or not. California outlaws peyote with no exceptions for NAC users. A famous case (*Woody, 1960*) exists where the charges against the NAC people were dismissed but the court was careful not to reject California's peyote ban in the process. Despite the Congressional action to protect rights of NAC peyote users, the existence of that state law has more recently been used against modern peyote users in California on the basis of state's rights. In the various cases involving the rights of other ethnicities, includ-

Pending religious freedom legislation

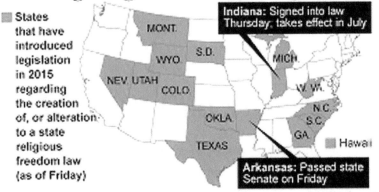

States that have introduced legislation in 2015 regarding the creation of, or alteration to a state religious freedom law (as of Friday)

Indiana: Signed into law Thursday; takes effect in July

Arkansas: Passed state Senate on Friday

Sources: National Conference of State Legislatures, AP   ©ChiTribGraphics

ing Europeans, to use peyote, the courts have almost consistently ruled against their participation with very few exceptions outside of the notable survival of James "Flaming Eagle" Mooney and the Oklevueha NAC. Most legal observers feel that Mooney benefited from a quirk of Utah law that has now been changed to prevent any one else from using it. It has been suggested that it is only a matter of time before it can be determined by the Feds how to undo that one step of "progress". One might count the Boyl case as a victory but closer reading will limit that in both importance and applicability.

Existing Religious Freedom Restoration Act (RFRA) Legislation (as of 2015)

Existing RFRA Legislation (as of 2015)

States with Excemptions for Peyote Use

State	Requirement
AZ	Sincere religious intent
CO	Within a bonafide religious organization
ID	Native Am descent within NAC ceremony on reservation
IA	Within NAC ceremony
KS	Within NAC ceremony with NAC membership, not incarcerated persons
MN	Within bonafide religious ceremony
NV	Within bonafide religious ceremony
NM	Within bonafide religious ceremony
OK	Within NAC ceremony
OR	Sincere religious intent
SD	Within bonafide religious ceremony
TX	Native American descent with NAC membership
WI	Within bonafide religious ceremony
WY	NAC membership.

Author Note: Discussion in this book regarding law are our own speculations and interpretations. We are not in a position to advise anyone in these matters.

PIPILZINTZINTLI

(Salvia divinorum, Coleus blumei and C. pumila)

A sacrament for divination and healing.

Other names: *yerba Maria, hojas de la pastora ("leaves of the shepherdess"), ska pastora.*

When psilocybe mushrooms and morning glories are not in season, the Mazatec Indians use the leaves of these plants of the Mint family (Labiatae) as substitutes. The effects occur more quickly, but are less striking and shorter-lasting (1-2 hours) than those of the mushroom.

Salvia divinorum

Coleus is an Old World introduction from southeastern Asia. Salvia has existed in Mexico since pre-Columbian times. Nevertheless, the Mazatecs recognized them as members of the same family. They regard *Salvia* as "the female," *Coleus pumila* as "the male" and two varieties of *C. blumei* as "the child" and "the godchild." None of these plants grow wild, but are cultivated by vegetative propagation usually in hidden places in remote and isolated mountain ravines.

When an Indian medicine man wishes to use this sacrament he kneels before the plant and prays to it, asking for its aid. Then he collects about seventy large leaves for each person taking the sacrament. In earlier times both the leaves and the stems were

Salvia divinorum

taken. Now only the leaves are used. This newer practice is less wasteful of nature's gifts because these plants are fairly rare and new leaves grow quickly where old ones have been removed. The leaves are sometimes thoroughly chewed and swallowed, but more often are crushed on a metate (usually by a virgin), diluted with a little water, strained and drunk. Except for the fact that the effects are of shorter duration any of the various ceremonial practices of the mush-, room and morning glory rites may be employed.

It is difficult to find *S. divinorum* even in Mazatec country. Coleus plants are available from any nursery or they can be raised from the seed. They are quite hardy as long as they get enough water and not too much hot sunlight. If they are clipped regularly they will branch out pro-fusely. The clippings can be placed in a glass of water until roots de-velop, and then replant-ed. Leaves which have fallen can be kept in a freezer for later use.

Salvia divinorum flower

They make excellent house plants and, if the flower stalks are re-moved before going to seed they can live indefinitely. The flower stalks may also be used sacramentally.

The active substance in these plants has not yet been identified. Another plant of the Mint family *(Lagochilus inebriens)* which is used as an intoxicant in central Asia, has similar effects. A psycho-active crystalline polyhydric alcohol has been isolated from the dried leaves of this plant. Our own experiments have indicated no psychoactive properties in the dried leaves of *Coleus* and *Salvia.* It is probable that the active substance is unstable.

PSILOCYBE MUSHROOMS
and related species
(Psilocybe mexicana **Heim**)

**A sacrament for probing the psychological
and psychic causes of illness, aiding in prophecy,
and for conducting a love feast.**

Other names: *teonanacatl ("flesh of God"), teyhuintli,
'nti si tho (Mazatec), sacred mushrooms, magic
mushrooms, ndi-shi-to (large species), ndi-qui-sho
(small species), "mushroom of superior reason"
(Psilocybe caerulescens var. nigripes). Crown of Thorns
mushroom (P. zapotecorum).*

T he *Psilocybe mexicana* mushroom and its psychoactive alkaloids, psilocybin and psilocin, are illegal in the United States. However, there are at least fifteen other species containing these alkaloids which grow in many places throughout this country. Their legal status is not clear to us at present. Assuming the probability that

Psilocyve sp.

drug prohibition has not been extended to cover all.of these we will consider their use as sacraments. These are: *Psilocybe baeocystis, P. caerulescens, P. caerulipes, P. cubensis var. cyanescens, P. cyanescens, P. pe/licuosa, P. quebec-*

Psilocybe gills

ensis, P. semilanceata, P. silvatica, P. strictipes, Conocybe cyanopes, Copelandia cyanescens, Panaeolus foenisecii, P. subbalteatus. Various species differ in potency. *Psilocybe caerulescens* is said to be the strongest.

Readers are warned to be certain of both federal and state laws regarding a sacrament before that sacrament is used. These are schedule 1 if they contain psilocybin and/or psilocin and they are illegal to cultivate or to possess or use.

We also warn against ingestion of specimens which have not been expertly identified. Many species of mushroom are deadly. When a mushroom which contains psilocybin and psilocin is broken the injured portion usually turns bluish within half an hour. However, this is not positive proof that the mushroom contains no dangerous substances. If one intends to gather wild mushrooms for sacramental purposes, he should thoroughly understand the use of botanical identification keys, and consult them carefully. Combination of the key and the bluing test gives one a greater degree of certainty about identification.

There have been no reports of toxicity in the mushrooms listed above with the exception of *P. baeocystis.* In 1960 the death of

Magic Mushroom

a six-year-old boy was attributed to the ingestion of a large number of these. This species contains baeocystin alkaloids, and it was believed at the time but there was actually no proof that the death did not involve other mushrooms or factors due to the rapidity of death. Stamets and Ott both discussed that. I am guessing THIS text pulled their info from Cunningham's "Magical and Ritual Uses of Herbs"? JW Allen added an interesting note on the subject on his website:

"In the mid to late 1960s, two young children, both six years old reportedly died after allegedly consuming Psilocybe baeocystis. However, photographs given to the author by the physcians involved in the subsequent attempted treatment and later death of these children, one in Washington and a second reported death in California, were identified by (JWA) as Psilocybe cyanescens. In both incidents, entire families had also consumed these mushrooms and did not die. Because of this misidentification by the late Chicago mycologist Rolf Singer and Alexander H. Smith who noted the species in their 1958 monograph on the genus Psilocybe, numerous mushroom field guides for both edible and psilocybian mushrooms described it as a very dangerous and toxic mushroom which could cause death. Over the years, few authors have corrected this error in reporting the correct identification of the species as Psilocybe cyanescens." According to at least one commentator, the kids died rapidly from hyperthermia and seizures which suggests more was involved than was actually determined.

Once live psilocybin-bearing mushrooms have been obtained the mycelium (subterranean mat) can be grown from spores or any portion of the mushroom, on a sterilized potato-dextrose-yeast-agar culture in cotton-stoppered bottles. The mycelium contains as much psilocybin as the carpophores and can be grown in 14 days or less.

These mushrooms are employed sacramentally by the Maza-tec Indians in the highlands of southern Mexico—especially in the mountain village of Huautla de Jiménez in the state of Oaxaca. Fresh mushrooms appear there only during the summer rainy season. They are never sold by legitimate curanderos, but are offered freely during various rites. The ritual use of psilocybe mushrooms may vary from one curandero to another and depending upon the purpose. Often elements of Christianity are included.

The mushrooms are usually gathered on the mountainside by a virgin before sunrise at the time of the new moon. They are wrapped in banana leaves ta^ conceal them from irreverent eyes and taken to the church where they are placed in a gourd bowl at-- the altar while God's blessing is invoked. One ceremony reported was quite simple and lacking in ritual. The mushrooms were col-

lected, taken to the church, and then brought home. The person seeking help took the mushrooms, but the curandero did not. A restricted diet and sexual abstinence were required of the mushroom eater for four days before and four days after the ceremony. Pork,

Harvest

chicken, salt, fat and alcohol were not allowed during this period. During the ceremony the seeker—aided by the curandero—attempted to understand his problem.

A description given for a prophecy ritual is somewhat more involved. Before the ceremony a chocolate beverage was served. Women sang, danced and clapped hands. The curandero gathered some maize kernels, parrot feathers, cacao beans, copal resin, green tobacco and bark paper. He had fasted since noon of the preceding day. For five days he had abstained from sex, alcohol, meat and salt. This will continue for another five days. Otherwise he believes that he risks going mad. At sunset the altar candles are lit. Those present are seated on the floor. The question for prophecy is decided and clarified. The curandero arranges his paraphernalia before him. The mushrooms are eaten in pairs during a period of one hour. As many as 14 may be taken. No one is allowed to leave. Silence is maintained. The bark of a nearby dog could ruin the ceremony. The curandero rubs green tobacco on his head and stomach and on the back of his neck. He blows out the candles. At one a.m. the prophecy begins.

Growing magic mushrooms

Often the mushroom is taken as a sacrament for a love feast. Each adult takes either 4, 5, 6 or 13 pairs of mushrooms and experiences his own inner ecstasy while sharing feelings of brotherly love with the others. The curandero may chant or dance periodically during the event.

Sometimes the mushrooms are employed as a catalytic sacrament for depth analysis of psychologically or psychically induced illness. It is the belief of the Mazatecs that bad actions result in psychic disruption, pain and susceptibility to sorcery. The session is conducted by the male-venda, a curandero with special experience and intuitive talents in depth probing. At twilight the male-venda steals silently and secretly along unpeopled paths toward the patient's hut. If weak-spirited people should see him, sorcerers might learn of this through them and attempt interference with his work. The patient lies in the center of the room. Copal resin incense is burning. Only children and elders past the age of desire are allowed to be present as witnesses. The male-venda commends the patient to the care of various saints. He invokes the chiccoun (nature spirits) to have pity for the patient so that the mushrooms will bring him good rather than harm. Silence must be maintained by the witnesses lest the patient go mad. At midnight the male-venda snuffs the candles. He places two mushrooms in the patient's mouth and takes four himself. After these have been thoroughly chewed and swallowed two more are given to the patient while the male-venda consumes eight. After the mushrooms have taken effect the male-venda asks the patient why he is ill. If the patient resists answering or says that he does not know, the male-venda may remind him that he alone knows, for the reason is inside of him. Step by step the male-venda discovers and releases the patient's blocks and may take him back to his infancy to find the root cause for his illness or susceptibility. After the session the male-venda may advise medicine, diet or a period of sexual abstinence.

The initial effects of these mushrooms are usually felt within 30 minutes after ingestion. Dilation of pupils and muscular relaxation to the point of flaccidity are among the first symptoms. This may be followed by hilarity, difficulty in concentration, and later by visual and auditory hallucinations, lassitude, alteration of time and space, and isolation from surroundings without loss of awareness. Peak occurs about *VA* hours after ingestion and the total experience lasts about six hours.

It is said that curanderos who consume the mushrooms frequently tend to age rapidly. At 35 or 40 they may appear old and wrinkled. For this reason many busy curanderos do not take the sacrament with their patients. Unlike peyote, the mushrooms are said to be capable of driving a person mad if certain precautions are not taken. For this same reason pregnant women do not consume the mushrooms.

SAN PEDRO

(Trichocereus pachanoi)

A sacrament for determining the cause of maladies or for protecting a house.

Other names: *San Pedrillo, agua-colla, giganton (Ecuadorian names), huando hermoso, huachuma, cardón (Peruvian names).*

This large, branched cactus is found in Peru and Andean Ecuador at various altitudes ranging from sea level to 9,000 feet above that, and usually on the western slopes. In this setting the columns may eventually achieve a height of 10 to 20 feet. There are several other cacti which have a similar appearance and have been mistaken for it even by skilled botanists.

The flesh of this cactus, beneath its thick skin, contains mescaline (about 1.2 grams per kilo of fresh material). This is the first of the published values to appear in Western print in 1959/1960 and was based on material purchased by Claudine Friedberg in the Huancabamba witches market. It is not at all representative of most West-

San Pedro

ern horticultural materials which are far more often a fifth or even a tenth as much. The concentration varies depending upon the location of its growth. Higher altitudes and rich mineral content of soil favor mescaline production. San Pedro also contains 3,4-dimethoxy-phenyl-ethylamine, 3-methoxy-tyramine and traces of other similar alkaloids. Several other species of *Trichocereus* from South

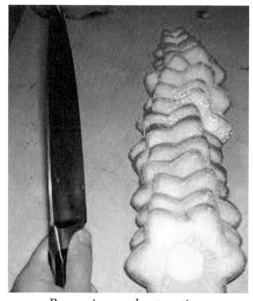

Preparing and extracting

America have been found to contain mescaline along with other related alkaloids. These are: *T. bridgesii, T. macrogonus, T. terscheckii,* and *T. werdermannianus.*

The psychopharmacological effects of San Pedro are similar to those of peyote because of the mescaline, but more tranquil because of the other alkaloids. The taste is less bitter than that of peyote and it has less tendency to produce nausea.

Witch doctors in Northern Peru prepare a hallucinogenic drink called "cimora" from San Pedro, Cereus

Preparing San Pedro Decoction

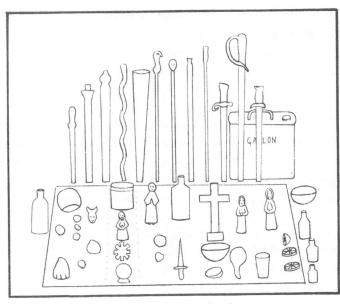

Arrangement of Curandero's Mesa

macrostibas (a cactus), Isotoma longiflora (containing lobeline), *Pedilanthus titimaloides* (Euphorbiaceae), and Datura stramonium (jimson weed). Cimora is used for diagnosis, therapy, divination, gaining control of another person's identity, and in the moon rites of the natives.

There is evidence that San Pedro cactus was employed in ritual and magic at least 3,000 years ago. Today it still plays a major role in folk healing as practiced by the curanderos (healers) of Northern Peru. Aside from its use as a diuretic and for external application to injuries and infections, it is the most important material used in the divination ritual for diagnosis and therapy of ailments.

At noon on the day of the ritual four pieces of the cactus are selected. These are about 12 inches long and 3 or 4 inches in diameter. Thin samples with seven ribs are usually chosen The rare four-ribbed ones are especially powerful in healing and may be sought out in difficult cases. The cacti are cut like bread slices about one-half inch thick and boiled in five gallons of water for seven hours. When this is done a small portion of the liquid is poured into a flask and set aside

The ritual is usually conducted out of doors. First the curandero lays out his mesa or altar table upon the ground. This is a woven mat about six feet by three feet. Upon this an altar cloth is placed. Behind the mesa is a row of twelve staffs or swords stuck in the ground. Starting from the viewer's far right when standing before the mesa (see diagram), the swords are known as (1) the Sword of St. James the Elder, (2) the Sabre of St. Michael the Archangel, (3) the Sword of St. Paul, (4) the Staff of the Virgin of Mercy, (5) the Hummingbird Staff, (6) the Greyhound Staff, (7) the Eagle Staff, (8) the Swordfish Beak Staff, (9) the Serpent Staff, (10) the Staff of the Single Women, (11) the Owl Staff, (12) Satan's Bayonet.

These swords or staffs divide the mesa into three zones representing the positive, negative and neutral forces of the universe. The area immediately before the first eight staffs is called the Field of Divine Justice (Campo Justiciero). This zone is governed by Christ. Upon it are placed various positive artifacts such as: a crucifix, icons of saints, holy water, perfumes, an exorcising rattle, stones, shells, sugar, limes, tobacco, and the can of San Pedro infusion.

The area directly in front of staffs 10, 11 and 12 is called the Field of the Sly Dealer (Campo Ganadero). This zone belongs to Satan and contains objects representative of negative magic such as stones and ceramic fragments from ancient ruins, a triton shell, a deer foot, and a flask of cane alcohol.

Just as the yin and yang of Oriental philosophy are divided by the Tao, the narrow zone in front of the Serpent Staff separates the positive and negative fields of the mesa. This neutral zone (Campo Medio) is gov-

San Pedro flower

erned by St. Cyprian, a sor-
cerer who converted to Christianity. In this area are placed
various neutral objects, or
objects with both positive
and negative live potentials
such as a jar of magic herbs,
a statue of St. Cyprian, for-
tune-telling devices, a mirror
and a bronze sunburst.

Some of these items are
found on every curandero's
mesa. Others are objects
which circumstance brought
to him and which he recognized for their positive, negative or neutral value.

*San Pedro
(Trichocereus pachanoi)*

The ceremony is performed on any night except Monday. On
this day, they believe, spirits in purgatory roam about. The first part
of the ritual is a preparatory ceremony involving chants, prayers,
invocation of Catholic saints, use of the shaman's rattle, purification of the mesa and San Pedro brew with three perfumes, and
imbibing of tabaco through the nostrils. Tabaco is/prepared indi-
vidually for each participant immediately before use. It consists of
wild tobacco leaves *(Nicotiana rustica),* San Pedro infusion (from
the flask that was set aside), sugar candy, lime juice, cane alcohol,
and two perfumes.

At midnight all present must drink a cup of San Pedro infusion. The curandero drinks first; his assistants last. While the
curandero chants, all focus their attention on the neutral zone of
the mesa. One of the swords or staffs is then supposed to vibrate,
indicating the nature of the patient's illness. The curandero then

knows what evil he must exorcise. The patient, aided by the assistants, takes the staff and raises it to his face while imbibing tabaco or one of the ingredients (as indicated by the curandero) through his nostrils. One of the assistants cleanses the patient by rubbing his entire body with the staff. Then he makes slicing gestures in the air with the staff and taking one of the tabaco ingredients into his mouth sprays the staff and returns it to its place at the mesa. If at any point in the ritual the patient seems to be under attack, the curandero takes a sword and charges the "attacker" in the outskirts of the circle of people. Then holding the sword-in both hands with the sharp edge away from him he performs seven somersaults— four one way and three perpendicular to that to form a cross. After the assistant has returned the vibrating staff to its place the curandero performs a purification ceremony. It is now about 4 a.m. and the ritual is concluded.

San Pedro and other mescaline-containing Trichocereus cacti are apparently legal to grow in the United States. In California the peyote law includes the Lophophora genus only but federal law outlaws mescaline consumption and use in any form. Peyote is illegal to grow anywhere in the USA without first obtaining a cultivation permit from the DEA.

SINICUICHI
(Heimia salicifolia)
**A sacrament for delving into the past and
remembering forgotten things.**

Other names*: abre-o-sol ("sun opener"), herva de la
vida ("herb of life"; Brazil), Heimia myrtifalia (either a
closely related species or a geographical variant
of H. salicifolia).*

This plant of the Loosestrife family (Lythraceae) may be found in the highlands of Mexico, but ranges south to Uruguay, Paraguay and Northern Argentina. In South America it .s
mostly employed in physical medicine, but in Mexico it is also valued for its mind-altering properties. Its major active alkaloid is cryogenine,$C_{24}H_{23}N_{03}(0\text{-}CH_3)_2$.

To prepare it for use as a mind sacrament the leaves are allowed to wilt slightly. Next they are ground on a metate (stone grinding board) and macerated in water. This juice is permitted to ferment a little and clarify in the sun for a day. Then is it drunk.

Heimia salicifolia

Heimia salicifolia

The effects of drinking it are: mild intoxication, slight giddiness, darkening of vision, auditory (but not visual) hallucinations, diminishing of sounds from the mundane world (sounds seem to be distorted and coming from a distance), pleasant drowsiness, slowed motion, cooling of the body, analgesia, skeletal muscle relaxation, slowing of heart beat, dilation of coronary vessels, enhancement of epinephrine, noncompetitive inhibition of acetylcholine and slightly reduced blood pressure. No hangover or unpleasant after-effects are experienced. If one has overindulged he may notice a golden-yellow tinge to everything on the following day.

Occasional, moderate use can enhance memory during intoxication. Many users have recalled very early events in great detail. Some even claim to have tapped prenatal events. Habitual and excessive use of sinicuichi can eventually hinder and confound the memory processes. It should be used only when recollection of lost events cannot be otherwise accomplished.

When employing sinicuichi as a mental sacrament one should prepare himself through meditation to relax and open the mind and senses. Light eating or even fasting on the day of use is recommended. While waiting for the draught to take effect one should gently contemplate the material he is trying to recall. If remembrance is stubbornly evasive, it should not be pursued relentlessly. The subconscious memory banks do not favor too much pressure. It is better in this case to turn the thoughts to other things for a while or to relax and let thoughts flow. The missing recollections will usually come of their own if this is done.

We know of no local source of sinicuichi at this time. It must be sought in Mexico or South America, either where it grows or from herb vendors in the marketplaces. If only the dried herb is available, this can be steeped (not boiled) in hot water and allowed to sit for a day in the sun before drinking. The individual must find the correct amount to use for himself. We suggest that no more than a heaping tablespoonful of the dried material or the equivalent in fresh herbs be taken as a first experimental dose.

SOMA

(Amanita muscaria)

Other names: *asumer, amrita (both Aryan), pong, pongo, pank (Siberian tribes), bolond gomba (Magyar), Narren Schwamm (German), fly agaric (English).*

The scientific world now generally agrees with the findings of R. Gordon Wasson that the mysterious Soma of the Aryans, who established themselves in the Indus Valley over 3,500 years ago, was principally *Amanita muscaria.* More than 1,000 hymns of the Rig Veda are dedicated to this hallucinogen.

This mushroom of the Agaric family (Agaraceae) grows in the north temperate parts of the Eastern and Western hemispheres. It is easily recognized by its brilliant red caps and white warts. Although it grows abundantly, it is not always easily discovered: It usually occurs in birch or pine forests since these trees are its natural hosts. To find it one must determine its season in his locale and look beneath dense layers of leaves or needled.

The active substances in this mushroom are muscimol, a hallucinogen affecting the central

Amanita muscaria

Aminita was gathered by the light of the Moon

nervous system, and ibotenic acid, a precursor of muscimol which appears to have more physical toxicity rather than psychological activity in that it causes flushing of the skin, lassitude, and possible migraine hangover. These fungi also contain muscazon, muscaradine and muscarine. The latter, a psychoactive, but dangerously toxic alkaloid, was at one time believed to be responsible for the mental effects of the mushroom. It is now understood not to be so because of the relatively small amount present and the difficulty with which this molecule passes the blood-brain barrier.

A close relative of *A. muscaria* known as panther caps *(A. pantherina)* contains large quantities of muscarine. Many Amanita users prefer the pantherina due a claim of better activity and fewer side effects. *A. pantherina* has an appearance similar to *A. muscaria,* but is brown or yellow, not red. Several other species of *Amanita—A. virosa, A. verna* and *A. phalloides* (destroying angel)—contain even more lethal substances.

A. muscaria has been used for centuries by the Koryaks, Kamchadals and Chukchis (Esquimo tribes of the Siberian Peninsula) for ritualistic and shamanistic purposes as well as for pleasurable revelry. Their usual method of preparation is to collect the mush-

Dried Amanita muscaria

rooms during the warm season and hang them on a string like beads to dry in the sun or near a fire. Drying is done to increase the potency and reduce some of their toxicity. This act is backed by scientific fact. The somewhat toxic ibotenic acid is converted to psychoactive muscimol by water loss and decarboxylation during drying. Properly dried mushrooms may have twice as much muscimol as fresh ones and considerably less ibotenic acid. Mushrooms which have dried unplucked in the ground are believed to be most potent. Also smaller, deep colored specimens are said to be more powerful than larger, paler ones.

A woman of these northern tribes does not partake of the amanita unless she is a shaman. Among the Koryaks the women prepare the mushrooms for their men by moistening and softening them in the mouth and rolling them in the hands into sausage-shaped morsels. The men either chew these or swallow them whole. Usually three agarics are taken: one large and two small. Sometimes ten or twelve are eaten, but this could easily be a lethal dose. Often they are added to soups, sauces, reindeer milk or bogberry (similar to blueberry) juice. The Kamchadals prepare a wine by fermenting a mixture of amanita and bogberry juice.

If anyone wishes to use *A. muscaria* as a sacrament, we suggest that its identity be confirmed by an experienced mycologist, and that he take no more than one modest-size mushroom. The Siberian tribesmen have a far more robust constitution than most of us.

One of the more curious facets of amanita pharmacology is that after a person has become intoxicated most of the psycho-active muscimol is passed into the urine while much of the more dangerous components is apparently metabolized into harmless substances. The Siberians have long been aware of this phenom-enon. Those who cannot obtain the mushrooms collect the urine of intoxicated tribesmen and by drinking it become intoxicated themselves. Often a person imbibes his own urine to maintain his state of inebriation. This recycling can be repeated four or five times before the potency finally dwindles out. In shamanistic ritu-als Yukaghir witch doctors drink muscimolated urine prior to eat-ing the mushrooms. The effects of amanita vary with the individ-ual and with the mushrooms depending upon location of growth, drying method, and amount taken. The usual course, however, is: twitching, dizziness and possible nausea about half an hour after ingestion followed soon by numbness of the feet. At this point a person will frequently go into a half-sleep state for about two hours. He may experience colored visions and be aware of sounds around him but it is usually impossible to rouse him. After this a good-humored euphoria may develop with a light-footed feeling and perhaps an urge to dance. At this time a person often becomes capable of greater than normal feats of strength. Next hallucina-tions may occur. Objects may appear larger than they are. Some-times a person may feel compelled to reveal harbored feelings. The post-sleep stage may last three or four hours.

Little is known about the amanita practices of the Aryans ex-cept for that which can be discerned from the Vedic hymns. The mushroom was gathered at night by the light of the full moon. The juice was pounded out, filtered through a woolen cloth, mixed with water, milk, honey, or a barleycorn infusion, and drunk during magical and religious rites. There is some indication that the ancient Aryans were aware of the urine-drinking phenomenon as evidenced by the following quotes from the Rig Veda.

Quotes from the Rig Veda.

> *Like a stag, come here to drink! Drink Soma, as much*
> *as you like. Pissing it out day by day, O generous one,*
> *You have assumed your most mighty force.*

VII 4.10

> *Soma, storm cloud filled with life,*
> *Milked with milk and butter,*
> *Navel of the Path; Immortal Concept,*
> *Which springs to life far from here*
> *In unison those charged with the task,*
> *The blessed do honor to Soma.*
> *In flowing movements swollen men piss Soma.*

IX 74.4

> *In the belly of Indra*
> *Intoxicating Soma is filtered.*

IX 80.3

The Vedic poets speak of three filters involved in the preparation of Soma. The first, it appears, is the filtering of sunlight into the mushroom, bearing its magical powers from the heavens.

The second, no doubt, is the woolen cloth through which the juices were strained. It is probable that the third filter was the human organism (possibly that of a priest) through which the liquids were passed.

The standard antidote for muscarine poisoning is atropine. *A. muscaria* contains relatively little muscarine, so this antidote is useful mainly when one of the other toxic amanitas have been taken by error. Because atropine is also a poison it should be administered by professional or experienced persons. The Koryaks say that if too much agaric has been taken— leading to pressure on the stomach—two or three tablespoons of fat, oil, butter or blubber is an effective remedy. Some tribes believe that a swig of vodka is also helpful in these circumstances. We have no scientific data concerning either of these possibilities, but it is probable that these people know something about coping with amanita poisoning after several centuries of experience. If one of the more lethal amanitas *(phalloides, verna* or *virosa)* has been ingested there may be some chance of saving the victim's life if there is immediate medical attention.

YOHIMBE

(Corynanthe yohimbe)

A love sacrament for solemnizing matrimony, for occasional use before sexual intercourse, and for increasing psychic energy.

Other names: *Pausinystalia yohimbe, yohimbehe, johimbe.*

This tree of the family Rubiaceae is native to tropical West Africa, especially the French Congo and the Cameroons. For centuries the bark of the yohimbe tree has had a famous place in African folk medicine. Among Bantu-speaking tribes it is used as a stimulant and aphrodisiac.

Yohimbe tree

A decoction is made by boiling the shaved inner bark in water for half an hour or more. This liquor may be drunk upon a single occasion for its stimulating qualities, or small but gradually increasing doses may betaken over a period of ten to fifteen days. Some people find that the latter

Rauwolfia serpentina

procedure has a cumulative effect which greatly augments their erotic and psychic energies for some time after the series has been discontinued. Both yohimbe bark tea and pure yohimbine powder (yohimbine hydrochloride) have been used for this purpose.

The active constituents of yohimbe are yohimbine, yohimbiline, and related alkaloids. Yohimbine, the major alkaloid (also called quebrachine), is often available in its hydrochloride form, which makes it assimilable via mucous membranes when snuffed or applied beneath the tongue.

Yohimbine is a sympathomimetic indole-type alkaloid with both cholinergic and adrenergic blocking properties. It is also a serotonin inhibitor. Some scientific literature describes it as a hypertensive (increaser of blood pressure) while others say it is a hypotensive (decreaser of blood pressure). Our own findings are that it can be either depending upon the disposition of the body at the time and the stage of the experience. It is also a central stimulant and an activator of the spinal ganglia which affect the erectile tissue of the penis and clitoris. A man who has taken yohimbine may find himself having many spontaneous erections.

If one drinks yohimbe tea the first effects may be felt after 45 minutes. If ascorbic acid (vitamin C) 500 mg is added to each cup the effects are felt within ten minutes. This is probably because the alkaloid reacts with the acid to produce an ascorbate, which is more readily assimilated. If yohimbine HCl is snuffed, the effects are almost immediate. The first effects may be mild psychic changes, subtle perceptual changes without hallucinations, emotional stimulation, tears and running nose. Warm shivers through the spine may be experienced if the body is rested and in vigorous health. If energies are low these shivers may seem cold. The warm shivers or currents of neuron energy may be quite pleasurable, especially during sexual intercourse. The couple may experience sensations of their bodies and energies melting into one another. Orgasm is often intensified.

Yohimbine has stimulating properties similar to cocaine. Often one cannot sleep for many hours after taking the substance. If yohimbine HCl is snuffed one may even feel a numbing of the teeth like that caused by cocaine. Yohimbine does not have the addicting and septum-damaging properties of cocaine. Usually one does not feel as wired with yohimbine as he might with cocaine. Sometimes, however, it may act as an activator of anxiety. Both sodium amobarbitol and Librium alleviate this state, whereas imipramine can make the anxiety worse.

One should not use yohimbine if he has an active kidney ailment or injury, or any liver disorder. Neither

Aspidosperma quebrachoblanco

should yohimbine be taken with strong alcohol because this potentiates its toxicity to a very dangerous degree. It has been our own accidental experience that the combination of yohimbine with amphetamines can produce very unpleasant side effects. In three separate instances 20-30 mg yohimbine HCl had been snuffed by individuals whose ages ranged from 20 to 29. One had injected methedrine 10 hours earlier, another had taken a 5 mg. dexedrine tablet 3 hours earlier, and the third had taken a dexamyl diet pill 6 hours earlier. In each case the subject developed violent, uncontrollable shivers and apparent b.p. drop (hypotension) within 15 minutes after snuffing the yohimbine. These were accompanied by rapid, fluttery heart and pulse beat and breathing difficulties with feelings of pain and pressure on the chest during inhalation. The symptoms were most pronounced and longer-lasting in the subject who had injected methedrine. Yohimbine should not be combined with a host of assorted drugs. Much more study of drug pharmacology is needed.

We recommend that if one intends to take yohimbe or yohimbine, he should not have had any type of amphetamine within at least 24 hours. We must also warn against hidden amphetamines often used to spike street drugs such as LSD and cocaine. One should also be well-nourished, rested, and in good health. Common doses range between 15 and 50 mg., but we recommend that much less be used to start. We also recommend that booster doses not be taken when initial effects begin to subside, that it not be used more often than once every few weeks, and that it not be used so often as an intensifier of sexual feelings that dependency is created.

Yohimbine and/or related isomers are also found in other *Corynanthe* species, *As-*

Yohimbe Molecule

Yohimbe Bark

pidosperma que-brachoblanco, *Mytragyna stip-ulosa,* and *Rau-wolfia serpentina* (Indian snake-root—source of reserpine). How-ever, *Rauwolfia serpentina* is out of place here de-spite containing yohimbine and is not a suitable choice to ingest if wanting yohimbine as its major alkaloid is reserpine.

The use of that plant *could* potentially result in death either from being combined with stimulants, SSRIs or MAOIs or a variety of other drugs, or from the user's own hand following induced suicidal depression. Ghandi is reputed to have liked drinking *Rauwolfia* as leaf tea. Interestingly, it might have helped him stay nonreactive to confrontation. Its use rapidly and directly leads to neurotransmitter depletion (which is part of why it works, it is a profoundly effective neurotransmitter releaser that probably has a nice feeling onset). In short, it is not be recommended, especially novices.

A WEDDING CEREMONY WITH YOHIMBE AS A SACRAMENT

Yohimbe beverage and pure yohimbine have served as matrimonial sacraments in several marriages solemnized within the Church of the Tree of Life. Here are some guidelines for performing a wedding service. The nature of the ceremony, the readings and vows should reflect the beliefs and sentiments of the bride and groom, and should be decided between them with the assistance of the minister.

Much of the ceremony may be founded upon the combined cultural traditions, eclectic adaptations and personal beliefs of the bride and groom. Certain elements such as the presence of the best man and maid of honor, the giving away of the bride, the standard wording of the vows, and the placing of a ring on the bride's finger are customary but not absolutely necessary. The couple should inquire with the local marriage license bureau to find out what the state and city marriage requirements are.

The usual requirements are: a blood test (allow several days for results), the payment of a fee to the license bureau (usually about $2), the filling out of

Yohimbe enhances romance

the license and solemnization certificate, and the witnessing of the solemnization. The solemnization can be performed by any priest, minister, rabbi, or other church leader whom the couple selects. Or, if the couple wishes to dispense with religious connotations, it may be performed by any judge or justice of the peace in the presence of a witness. After performance of the matrimonial rites the solemnization certificate must be sent to the license bureau. A copy is filed and the original is returned to the couple.

When a marriage is performed within the Church of the Tree of Life the couple may design their own ceremony. If they leave this task to the minister, he should describe the intended ceremony, readings and vows to them for their approval. The wording of the vows should express the marital ethics of the couple rather than those of the society in which they live.

For a reading most modern couples prefer something brief and meaningful. It may be drawn from either religious or non-religious literature or composed by the person performing the service if he has that talent and inspiration.

The following is an example of a modern wedding ceremony appropriate to the sentiments and beliefs of the Tree of Life Church. It is intended as a set of suggestions and need not be followed with any degree of exactness. If anything approaching a standardized ceremony for matrimony or any other occasion is ever adopted by the Church, it will have to evolve from the people rather than be imposed by the founders and directors.

Authored by Michael Marinacci
Reprinted by permission

The Church of the Tree of Life

A s the 1960s drew to a close, the Brotherhood of Eternal Love and other psychedelic sects remained outlaw organizations. Their sacraments of choice – LSD and cannabis – were more popular than ever as recreational drugs, but were still highly illegal, lacking the unique protected status of peyote within the Native American Church. Threatened with harsh legal penalties for mere possession, much less open usage, of the hallucinogens, spiritually-oriented trippers became far more circumspect and considerably less idealistic about their inner explorations.

Frustrated by the situation, many in the psychedelic underground began gathering information about psychoactive substances that had remained legal. Eventually a small book called *Legal Highs* was published that described a cornucopia of plants, fungi and synthetics that packed the mind-altering punches of the better-known drugs, but were licit and relatively easy to obtain. Published by a Manhattan Beach-based firm, and written as a taxonomy-style handbook, *Legal Highs* described the names, active ingredients, usage, effects and contraindications of materials ranging from LSD-like Hawaiian Baby Woodrose seeds, to mescaline-bearing San Pedro cactus, to the African aphrodisiac Yohimbe. It became an underground bestseller, and can today be found online as a public textfile, its information still used by self-styled 21st century alchemists

Legal Highs and similar works publicized obscure but non-proscribed psychedelic drugs. In *Legal Highs'* introduction, author

Adam Gottlieb stated, "It may be of some interest to some readers that the Church of the Tree of Life has declared as its religious sacraments most substances in this book.Because these substances were legal at the time of the Church's inception and incorporation, their use cannot be denied to members through any future legislation without directly violating the Constitution's guarantee of religious freedom."

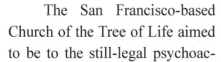

The San Francisco-based Church of the Tree of Life aimed to be to the still-legal psychoactive substances what the Native American Church was for peyote. Incorporated in 1971 by life-extension expert John Mann, it existed largely as a legal entity to protect the use of the drugs mentioned in *Legal Highs*. If any of these materials became illegal, it was reasoned, a religious-use exemption for Church members could be grandfathered in with the new statutes, much as the peyote exemption had been for American Indians.

Unlike the Native American Church, the Church of the Tree of Life had neither ethnic strictures for membership, nor set theological doctrines. Spiritually libertarian, it maintained that the psychoactive substances were God's gifts to humanity, and that consenting adults had the right to use them in whatever manner they desired, so long as their actions didn't impinge on the rights of others. The Church didn't officially recognize LSD, cannabis or other Schedule One drugs as sacraments, but promulgated the use of legal alternatives like morning glory seeds, kava, calamus root, damiana, and other non-proscribed substances as tools for consciousness expansion. Membership was open to anyone who agreed with these general principles; an SASE sent to Church headquarters on Columbus Avenue in San Francisco would return with a membership card and the latest issue of Bark Leaf, the Church newsletter.

The Church of the Tree of Life described its Eucharistic entheogens in a little book called *The First Book of Sacraments*. Published a year before *Legal Highs*, it not only anticipated much of the practical information in that work, but also discussed the importance of ritual practice as a way to sanctify using the substances and to gain spiritual wisdom. The book also featured an essay on "Sacraments and Magic" by Frater C.A., which examined the use of the drugs in the context of Western ritual magick. A list of suppliers was included as well.

One of the Church's prime sacramental sources was the Inner Center of Hermosa Beach. A popular item in its mail-order catalog was 5-MeO-DMT, a legal variant of the short-acting tryptamine DMT, which produced a brief yet powerful psychedelic trip. The chemical was sprayed onto parsley or oregano leaves, which would then be smoked like marijuana to produce an intense, almost otherworldly state.

Another big seller was morning-glory seeds, offered in an untreated state (the seeds contained a close chemical relative of LSD, and many seed companies had taken to spraying them with methyl mercury to prevent spoilage and/or discourage trippers). Perhaps influenced by the Church, around this time California hip-culture fair vendors began to offer "Utopian Bliss Balls," Medjool dates packed with lysergic Hawaiian baby woodrose seeds and herbal supplements, as a legal psychedelic alternative to the infamous Orange Sunshine tablets that the Brotherhood of Eternal Love had handed out at rock festivals and hippie festivals just a few years earlier.

By 1972, the Church claimed 1,500 members. Although many joined mainly to obtain the promised legal status as entheogenic religionists, as well as connections for non-proscribed drugs, some members took the psychedelic path quite seriously, and sought to create rituals that would reflect the sect's non-denominational, counterculture sensibilities. Impressed by the aesthetics of Mexico's peyote-eating Huichol Indians, some Bay-Area Tree of Lifers tried to

First edition of The First Book of Sacraments

develop a ritual that would combine the Huichol's creativity with the spiritual power of Native American peyotism. Not much came of the efforts – one Church member told psychedelic researcher Peter Stafford that the resulting rite was "somewhat hokey," and didn't capture the essence of the hallucinogenic vision quest.

Largely because it remained relatively small and low-key, and concerned itself mainly with obscure psychoactives that lacked the notoriety of the Schedule One drugs, the Church of the Tree of Life survived well into the 1980s unmolested by the War on Drugs or popular opprobrium. But most of the post-Sixties psychedelic culture was just too closeted and individualistic to maintain a stable, organized religious institution dedicated to the mind-expanding experience, and the sect vanished around 1990. Still, the work it did investigating legal entheogens, and their use in sacred contexts, lived on in such academic groups as the Multidisciplinary Association for Psychedelic Studies (MAPS) and the Council on Spiritual Practices (CSP), which treated hallucinogens as powerful, life-changing substances worthy of study. And much of the Internet-based public-domain information about both legal highs and psychedelic spirituality can be traced to the Church's pioneering efforts in publicizing consciousness expansion through little-known psychoactive substances – scraps of the Flesh of the Gods that had somehow escaped John Law's notice.

- -

Reprinted from: Califias Blogspot, November 2014

http://califias.blogspot.com/2014/11/the-church-of-tree-of-life.htmlSunday, November 2, 2014

RECOMMENDED READING

Aberle, David F. *The peyote religion among the Navaho.* Chicago: Aldine, 1966.

Allegro, John M. *The sacred mushroom and the Cross.* New York; Bantam, 1971.

Brand, Stuart. The Native American Church meeting. *Psychedelic Review* 9 (1967).

Britton, N. L., and Rose, J.N. *The Cactaceae: descriptions and illustrations of plants yf the cactus family.* Washington, D.C.: Carnegie Institute.

Castaneda, Carlos. *The teachings of Don Juan: a Yaqui way of knowledge.* New York: Ballantine Books, 1969. *A separate reality: further conversations with Don Juan.* New York: Simon & Schuster, 1971.

Clark, W. G., and delGiudice, J., eds. *Principles of Psycho-pharmacology.* New York: Academic Press, 1970.

Clark, Walter Houston. *Chemical ecstasy—psychedelic drugs and religion.* New York: Sheed and Ward, 1969.

Dobkin (de Rios), Marlene. Trichocereus pachanoi: a mescaline cactus used in folk healing in Peru. *Economic Botany* 22: 191-94.

Downing, D. F. The chemistry of psychomimetic substances. *Quarterly Review* 16:133-62.

Efron, Daniel H., ed. *Ethnopharmacological search for psychoactive drugs.* Washington, D.C.: U.S. Govt. Printing Office, 1967.

Emboden, William. *Narcotic plants.* New York: Macmillan, 1972.

Enos, Leonard. *A key to the American psilocybin mushroom.* Lemon Grove, Calif.: Church of the One Sermon (1835 Lincoln St.), 1970.

Fadiman, James. Psychedelic properties of Genista canariensis. *Economic Botany* 19:383-84.

Fields, F. Herbert. Rivea corymbosa: notes on some Zapotecan customs. *Economic Botany* 23:206-9.

Furst, Peter T. Huichol conceptions of the soul. *Folklore Americas* vol. 27, no. 2, pp. 39-106.Ariocarpus retusus, the "false peyote" of Huichol tradition. *Economic Botany* 25:182-87. *Myth in art: a Huichol depicts his reality.* Los Angeles: Latin American Center, University of California, 1968.

Flattery, David S., and Pierce, J. M. *Peyote.* Berkeley, Calif.: Berkeley Press, 1965.

Genest, K.; Rice, W. B.; and Farmilo, C. G. Psychotomimetic substances in morning glory seeds. *Proceedings of the Canadian Society of Forensic Studies* 4:167-86.

Harding, A. F. *Ginseng and other medicinal plants.* Moke-lumne Hill, Calif.: Health Research, 1908.

Hoffer, A., and Osmond, H. *The Hallucinogens.* New York: Academic Press, 1967.

Hofmann, Albert. The active principles of the seeds of Rivea corymbosa and Ipomoea violacea. *Botanical Museum Leaflets, Harvard University,* 20:194-212.

Johnston, J. B. Elements of Mazatec witchcraft. *Ethnological Studies* 9:119-50.

Kluver, Heinrich. *Mescal and mechanisms of hallucinations.*

Chicago: University of Chicago Press, 1966.

La Barre, Weston. *The peyote cult.* New York: Schocken Books, 1969, 3ed.

Lewin, Louis. *Phantastica: narcotic and stimulating drugs.* London: Routledge and KeganPaul, 1964.

Malcolm, Andrew I. *The pursuit of intoxication.* New York:Washington Square, 1972.

McCleary, James A.; Sypherd, Paul S.; and Walkington, David. Antibiotic activity of an extract of peyote Lophophora williamsii. *Economic Botany* 14:247-49.

Neal, J. M., and McLaughlin, J. L. Cactus alkaloids. *Lloydia* 33:3.

Reti, L. Cactus alkaloids and some related compounds. *Fortschritted. Chem. Org. Naturst.* 6 (1950).

Robichaud, R. C; Malone, J. H.; and Schwarting, A. E. Pharmacodynamics of cryogenine, an alkaloid isolated from Heimia salicifolia. Part 1. *Archives Internationales dePharmaco-cynamie et Therapie,* 110:220-32.

Roseman, Bernard. *The peyote story.* Hollywood, Calif.: Wilshire Book Co., 1966.

Sato, P. T.; and Howard, W.H. Peyote alkaloids: identification in the Mexican cactus Pelecyphora aselliformis.Sc/eA7ce 176 (June 1972): 1131-33

Schultes, Richard Evans. The plant kingdom and hallucinogens. *Bulletin on Narcotics,* vol. 21 nos. 3, 4; vol. 22 no. 1. New York: United Nations, 1969,1970.

Shulgin, Alexander T. The narcotic pepper: the chemistry and pharmacology of Piper methysticum and related specias. *Bulletin on Narcotics,* 25, 2, 59-74.

Slotkin, James S. *The peyote religion.* Glencoe, Ill.: The Free Press. and McAllester, David P. Transcription and analysis of Menomini peyotism. (With text and music of peyote songs.)

Transactions of the American Philosophical Society, vol.42, part 4 (1952).

Steinmetz, E. F. *Piper methysticum (kava).* 347 Keizersgracht, Amsterdam, Neth., 1960.

TenHouten, Warren D., and Kaplan, Charles D. *Science and its mirror image: a theory of inquiry.* New York: Harper and Row, (spring 1973).

Tyler, Varro E., Jr. The physiological properties and chemical constituents of some   habit forming plants. *Lloydia* 29:275-92.

United States Code (1970 edition). Volume 5, Title 21. Washington D.C.: U.S. Govt. Printing Office, 1971..

Wasson, R. Gordon. *Soma: Divine Mushroom of Immortality,* new ed. New York: Harcourt Brace Jovanovich, 1971.

Wasson, Valentina P., and Wasson, R. Gordon. *Mushrooms, Russia and History.* New York: Pantheon, 1957.

9 781579 512101